The Friendship Tree

and Other Stories for Children by Children

Virginia Lynch Graf, Editor

Pamela Yourell, Illustrator

Vangar Publishers
Baltimore

Library of Congress: 93 - 94112

ISBN 1-882788-03-6

Published by: Vangar Publishers
420 Hillen Road
Baltimore, MD 21286

Printed and bound in the
United States of America

Printing: 6 5 4 3 2 1

Introduction

Stories for Children by Children is a unique concept reflecting a dream of Virginia and Robert Graf to encourage children to write creatively. Vangar Publishers was founded by the Grafs primarily to provide quality reading materials for families and to give opportunity for young writers.

A writing contest for children, ages 5 to 15, was conducted from November 15, 1992 to February 15, 1993 and the stories in this first collection were those chosen from among the entrants. The annual contest winners will be published each year.

In this first edition of *Stories for Children by Children* the reader will find wide variety. Entertainment is found in humor, friendship, suspense, nature and surprise. Pam Yourell's illustrations are sensitive to each writer and she captures the heart of every story. We hope you enjoy reading them as much as we did. Congratulations to the students; special thanks to their parents and teachers!

(Our own children's stories were not among the 20 winners. We included their stories to illustrate what very young children are able to do and because they couldn't understand why they had to be excluded.)

Contents

Stories

for Children

by Children

The Friendship Tree

by M. Beach Carey
Baltimore, Maryland
Grade 8, Maryvale Prep

When I was a little girl everyone called me Cat. Now people call me Catherine. My little sister's golden curls and angelic, baby blue eyes earned her the nickname, Curly. My big brother, Mikey wrestled with me and tickled Curly.

We lived in a stone house on Andover Way. A path of large, flat, stepping stones led to our front door. On the front lawn stood an ancient, weeping willow tree. We loved that tree, especially mother and me. Curly and I played together under that tree everyday after school.

"I love this tree," Curly told me one day. We were sitting under the willow having a tea party.

"I love it too," I agreed happily.

There was also a vegetable garden in the side yard. The garden provided us with cucumbers, carrots and tomatoes during the summer months. We felt content with the house, garden, and plush, green lawn.

Curly's friend, Karen lived next door and Mikey had friends all over the neighborhood. Mother and Dad were friends with the McCalls and the Jacksons, our neighbors. I also wanted a friend nearby. One day a new girl was standing under our tree.

"Who are you?" I asked the girl.

"My name is Patty; what's yours?" The girl was very friendly.

"My name is Cat. I'm nine. How old are you?"

"I'm nine too! We just moved in down the street," Patty explained.

"Well," I said excitedly. "Do you want to be friends?"

"Sure, that sounds great!" laughed Patty.

That summer Patty and I became best friends. We played for hours under our wonderful tree. Sometimes we sprayed each other with the hose or had tea parties with Curly. In the fall Patty and I played in the leaves or did our homework together under the willow. Patty and I became inseparable.

Soon Christmas vacation came. Patty and I were very happy for the holidays. Every day there was something new to do. On the day after Christmas, Patty came to our house.

"Hello Patty, come on in," said my mother. "How was your Christmas?"

"Well, okay, I guess." Patty looked very unhappy.

"Patty, what's wrong?" I asked.

"We're going to move AGAIN," she forlornly explained.

I couldn't believe it. My best friend was moving. We just got to really know each other and now she was leaving. I couldn't stand the thought of it.

Patty moved away in January. I was unhappy all winter and most of the spring. I wrote letters to Patty and she wrote back. She told me she lived near the seashore and liked to watch the waves, but there were no willow trees. Mother tried her best to make me feel happy but I missed Patty terribly. Sometimes I would sit under the willow tree remembering all the things Patty and I did together.

One day in late May while walking home from school, I was feeling particularly happy. Enjoying the warm sun, singing birds and blossoming spring flowers, I just felt it was going to be a great day. I was approaching our stepping stones when I saw someone hiding under the willow branches.

"Surprise!" called a familiar voice.

"Patty, Patty!" I cried. I couldn't believe it! I gave my best friend a hug.

"I've been waiting for you under the friendship tree," explained Patty.

"Oh, Patty, what a wonderful name for our tree," I said.

We spent the rest of the day catching up on news and feeling good about being together. Before we knew it, the day was over. We had to say good-bye again.

That was many years ago. Patty and I are still friends. Patty continues to live by the sea and I live in our house on Andover Way. The Friendship Tree has a thicker trunk and many more branches but it's still a special place for sharing with the best of friends.

Quitting

by Lara O'Neill,
Joppa, Maryland
Grade 8, Harford Day School

I walked wearily out of the pool area and a blast of fresh air blew back my parka hood, exposing my chlorine laden hair. Then recovering my hood and windblown hair, I jogged toward the car.

"Sorry to keep you waiting. You know Tom, he never lets us out on time. First, he gives the talk and then it's a two and a half hour workout."

I blurted all this out to Mom as I exhaustedly plopped into the seat beside her.

"It's only been forty minutes, that's pretty good for Tom," she replied.

Shannon's hand appeared from the back seat extending a bag toward me. I grabbed it and opened it slowly, knowing it was a snack from Tricia, my aunt. Everyday I find something to make me smile in these special bags. Today, I don't feel like smiling or even wondering about what it is. I simply opened it, too engrossed in my thoughts to be excited.

"How was swimming today?" Mom asked the fateful question.

Flustered for a moment, I gather my meager strength answering, "I wonder if it's worth it."

The car came to a jolting stop and the screeching brakes echoed down my spine.

"What does THAT statement mean? Why would you say that? Whatever happened?"

Mom was shocked and the rapid fire questioning was a way to relieve her feelings. She was obviously taken back to hear me utter such an atrocity. I had expected this reaction and had already rehearsed my next lines. In fact, during swimming practice I had role played this whole scene.

"Look, Mom, look at my past year's swimming! Ever since I turned twelve, I've gone no where, absolutely no where! All my friends are getting faster. Why should I break my neck at practice and not even gain a second faster? Tom's practices are gruelling and I'm not getting anywhere. Why should I stick with it; what is it getting me?" All my thoughts came tumbling out in one mad rush.

"Yes," Mom quietly said. "You have had a hard year but there is still time to achieve your goals."

Mom was trying to soothe me into thinking of the possibilities of a miracle. I would have none of it.

"Do you really think I can get Juniors? Mom, I'm four seconds off in the 100 free style, ... four whole seconds!"

I was crying now, tears streaming down my face. I felt them leaving a hundred little watery paths, but I didn't care.

"Four seconds! ... and in the beginning of the year Tom told me I should get a fifty-four ... and I ... I have yet to break fifty-seven."

"Lara, Lara, calm down," Mom tried to comfort me.

"I believe you can still do it," Mom continued. "You're right, something is different. Your killer instinct is gone. All you have to do is clear your mind. You can do it, Lara. The only thing holding you back is you. Like Tom said, you've become a head case, worrying too much. You can turn that around if you'll just believe in yourself."

"Mom, let's get real. My brain's not a slate, you know. I just can't write success on it and it happens. Can't you see, I've gone no where, accomplished nothing." Among sobs, feelings of anger and other emotions, I felt it hard to breathe.

"Fine then, quit," Mom uttered the ultimate threat.

I yearned to accept the dare. I wanted relief and no more pressure. I sat quietly for a while and Mom did too. Finally, she started up the motor. We drove home and without words Mom and I both knew that despite the tears, I would be back at practice tomorrow. It was as if driven by some unknown force to suffer the physical pain and the mental indecision. I would be back again ... and again ... and again.

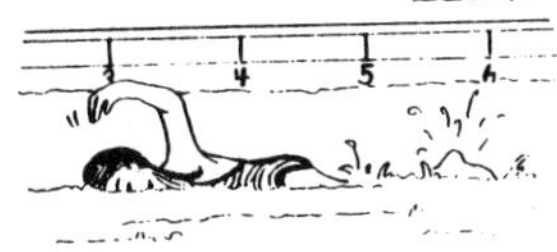

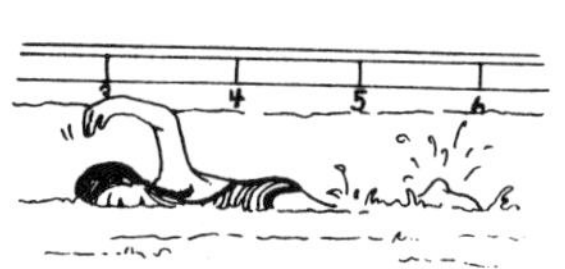

Convertible Confusion

By Robert A. Graf, Jr.
Towson, Maryland
Kindergarten, St. Pius X

Our family was traveling to Ocean City in our new, blue convertible. Daddy, Mama, my big sister and I were looking forward to a great vacation. It was a long way and we drove for hours. Rosie and I were getting bored. Dad made a new rule, no magic markers in the car. I guess he didn't like pictures in the old station wagon.

"Daddy, Mama, we finished the popcorn." Our snacks were already gone; the puzzle pages completed. We didn't know what else to do.

"How about counting convertibles?" Mom suggested. We decided to sing with our tapes instead.

Daddy pushed harder on the gas pedal because I really hate sitting too long. The little blue convertible started humming faster. We passed over lots of bridges and saw corn fields everywhere. Finally, we arrived at Ocean City.

Daddy parked our new car in the parking lot and then we helped unload a few of the bags.

"We'll unpack the rest later," Dad said.

Everyone wanted to swim so we rushed over to the swimming pool. Rosie and I have become pretty good swimmers. I like to dive and do back flips too.It was a hot day and we swam for most of the afternoon.

Later when we came back to the car, it was gone. We searched all over the hotel parking lot; no shiny convertible! We were all very upset. Dad decided it was best to call the police.

We called the police and they came quickly. They even brought a police dog. Dad gave them a clear report. For some reason it wasn't long before the police found our family car. It was still on the parking lot, the wrong parking lot. Our family had used another hotel's lot and then forgot where we parked! I think our new, little convertible had a big laugh.

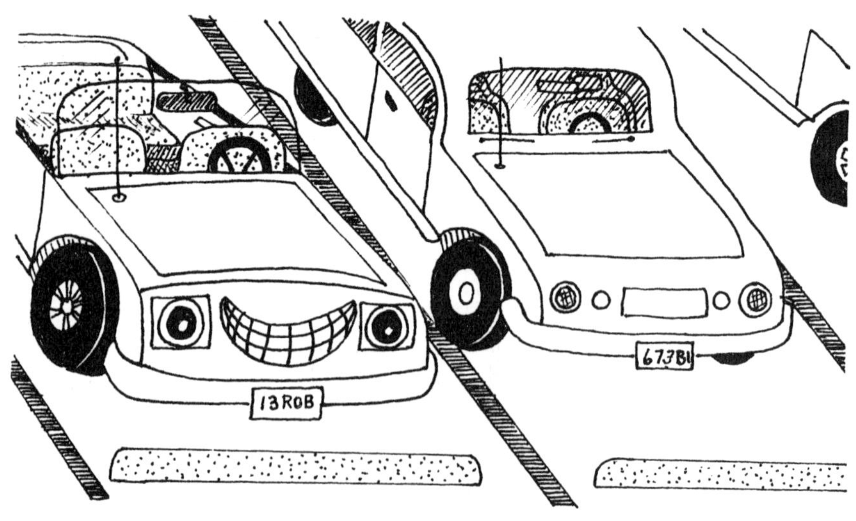

Despina to the Rescue

by Regina M. Niedzwicki
Baltimore, Maryland
Grade 8, St. Clement

The last thing a teacher wants is a class full of noisy and obnoxious seven year olds. Today Mrs. Patrick tries to control them but she can't because she has laryngitis. To add to the scene, cars are roaring down the road, rain is pouring and the thunder from the storm is shaking the whole school building. Having just finished lunch, the second grade boys show off for the girls who respond to their antics with high shrilled giggles.

"Do you like my new hot pink dress?" asks Despina.

"I love it," says Jennifer. "I wish I had one."

"Thanks, I got it yesterday along with a new Barbie that talks." Despina just about finishes when she is interrupted by Mrs. Patrick.

"Sit down, children," Mrs. Patrick desperately croaks.

"I dare you!" says Joe.

"Well, I double dog dare you!" exclaims Bobby.

"I triple dog dare you!" challenges Johnny.

Everyone's eyes are focused on Brian Ballton, the coolest guy in second grade. He is attempting a new stunt. He stands on a desk and laughs at Mrs. Patrick's pathetic sounds.

"Is he really gonna do it?" the girls whisper.

"Of course, I ain't chicken," states Brian.

"Oh isn't he wonderful," Brian's girlfriend, Julie sighs.

The class becomes silent as they hear the pop from the pen top. Brian then places the cap on the end of his saliva covered tongue. The children watch in amazement, mouths wide open, eyes alert. Bobby studies the clock to see how long Brian, atop the desk, can hold the cap on his tongue.

"Five minutes, he has held that cap for five minutes," Bobby screams.

"Brian must have done this before," he asserts. "It looks impossible unless, of course, he's been practicing."

Brian starts to laugh. " 'atch ith."

It was hard to understand what Brian said. He starts jumping from desk to desk, leaping and dancing as if the cap were glued to his tongue. Bobby and the other kids are laughing uproariously. Despina starts to get worried; she doesn't think jumping on desks with a pen cap is safe. It all happens so fast. Brian looses his balance.

"A-a-a-gh" he tries to yell. Everyone laughs louder. Brian is choking.

"Get out of the way," cries Despina as she pushes through the boys. "He's turning blue!"

"Oh come on, Despina, he's just faking!"

It was true Brian did joke around a lot but this time it was different. Mrs. Patrick also knew that Brian was in trouble.

"He's unconscious; he isn't breathing," squeaks Mrs. Patrick.

"Go get the nurse, somebody, quick!" She tries again to be heard.

"I can help," shouts Despina. " I know what to do; I'm going to be a nurse."

"Do something! Somebody do something," Mrs. Patrick is desperate.

Despina with the help of some of her classmates stands Brian on his feet. She quickly gets behind him and does the Heimlick Maneuver. Mrs. Patrick's eyes are as big as saucers. The cap shoots out of Brian's mouth but he is still unconscious.

Mrs. Patrick runs to call 911. While she calls, Despina starts to do CPR. Brian finally spits up covering Bobby's sneakers. Bobby looks at his repulsively coated shoes and finally stops laughing. He says to Brian, "What 'cha do that for?"

"What happened?" asks Brian.

"While you were showing off, you fell, hit your head and swallowed the cap," explains Despina.

The paramedics arrive. They check over Brian. He seems okay but they decide to take him into the emergency just as a precaution. Before they leave, they congratulate Despina.

"I don't know what to say," she shyly replies to their praise.

The class, now in shock, is finally subdued. Just then the sun starts to shine and Mrs. Patrick's voice comes back.

Later Despina was awarded a medal for saving Brian's life. The whole thing happened so quickly that some kids said it was like a miracle. Hopefully, Brian learned a lesson. Everyone in second grade agreed that God must have been very proud of Despina for doing such a brave deed.

The Never Ending Passage

by Kirstyn Fernandez
Fort Meade, Maryland
Grade 6, St. Augustine

It was a hot, June day in Eastern Pennsylvania. Despite the heat, Tamara rushed to Michelle's house. Michelle, her best friend, lived in a mansion with her wealthy parents, Mr. and Mrs. Carter. A butler invited Tamara inside and she waited anxiously for her friend to appear.

Finally, Michelle and Tamara were able to get down to the real reason for visiting.

"Let's play hide and seek," said Michelle. "You're it."

"One, two, three," counted Tamara, "seven, eight, nine, ten. Ready or not, here I come."

Michelle was hiding inside her bedroom closet. It was quite spacious. There were three shelves on the side wall and two bars for hanging clothes. She leaned against the back wall listening for her friend who was coming closer and closer. Suddenly the back wall gave in with a loud "click, crack, boom." Michelle fell backwards through the opening.

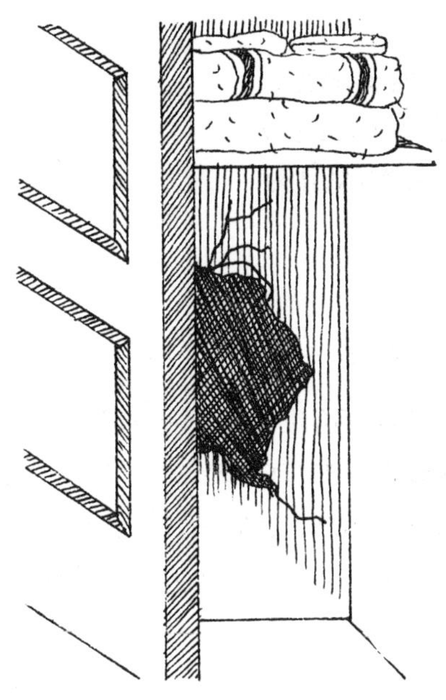

"Michelle, I heard that," Tamara sang out. "You must be in your room." She peered into the large closet; no Michelle. Because it was dim, she didn't notice a tiny faint outline of a board slowly closing. She moved away from the closet intent on finding Michelle.

"Okay, I give up; where are you?"

No sound. She looked around the hallway and then heard Michelle's Mom calling them for lunch. Still no answer.

"Meow," said Carrie, Michelle's cat. She was pawing around the closet.

After Mrs. Carter, Tamara and the house attendants had searched the whole house and couldn't find Michelle, Mrs. Carter called the police. Tamara told them about the noise she thought she heard earlier coming from the closet.

They knocked through one of the cupboard walls but found nothing.

"I'm sorry," Mrs. Carter, "there's no little girl here. She must have gone outside. We'll keep searching the neighborhood."

Then they added, "Your cat is upstairs in that mess we made and we couldn't get her to stay out of it."

"Little girl,"muttered Tamara,"that's Michelle."

Tamara raced home to grab some supplies: flashlight, hammer, and Dad's chisel. She went back to the mansion. She looked at the hole the police had made in the cupboard. Funny no one noticed that in the back of the closet there was a wooden panel with a middle board easily ready to be pried open. She decided to give it a hard pull.

"Tamara!" the butler was calling her. "Your mother wants you home now for dinner."

Tamara ate as fast as she could. Her mind was only on getting back to that closet and finding Michelle. She excused herself and asked if she could go back over to Michelle's.

"I don't think it's a good idea for you to bother the Carters. They're terribly upset. They don't need you around right now," said Dad.

"Give them some time," Tamara's mother sadly said.

Tamara was restless but she listened to her mother. She didn't go back to the mansion for a few days and finally she could stand it no longer. Mr. Carter opened the door himself. He had a sad, droopy look. Tamara was aghast as she looked at the mess in the house. It seemed as if Michelle's parents' grief was so overwhelming that nothing was done.

Quickly, Tamara went upstairs to the cupboard. Her tools were where she left them. She pushed the chisel under the loose board and it gave way easily. She was inside another room. It seemed to lead toward another room. Did Michelle come through here? Something caught her eye near the wall board, a small, shiny, hair bead. Her heart jumped. Again she pulled a board and found herself able to climb into another room.

This room had a few, furnishings. On the dresser in the corner was a dusty book entitled, *English Homes.* Tamara blew off the dust from the cover and started paging through the book. She couldn't believe her eyes. Inside the book was a picture of a house exactly like this one. She read on and discovered the house was two centuries old. It had once belonged to a rich man who had sealed off half the house for his riches and other treasures. The man died suddenly and no one knew more than that. Tamara was sure this was the house!

Tamara opened the drawers of the dresser. Jewelry of all kinds was neatly packed in elegant cases. She looked around for more. Gold, silver, and precious gems were tucked away in the other two drawers.

"Will you look at this?" she heard herself exclaiming. Then she remembered that she was looking for Michelle. She examined the walls looking for another entrance; sure enough, she found one. As she climbed into the next chamber, she heard, "Meow, meow."

"Come here, Carrie," Tamara called to the cat.

"You know where Michelle is, don't you, girl?"

Carrie ran past Tamara to a little waterfall.

"Don't expect me to go in there," said Tamara as she watched Carrie jump in and disappear through the falls to the floor below.

"Oh well, this is for Michelle," said Tamara as she too splashed through the tiny falls. Tamara and the cat found themselves in a hallway. No more wooden boards to pull but rather many doors.

"Which one, Carrie?" asked Tamara.

"Meow," was the only answer.

"I guess I'll have to figure it out," said Tamara.

Every doorway was dusty and dark but dim light seemed to be coming from under one door. Slowly and cautiously, Tamara opened the door. Inside she saw clothes hanging , Michelle's clothes!

"Where was Michelle?" She looked at what appeared to be a cupboard door and opened it. It was a bedroom and there was Michelle. Tamara woke her with a rush of questions.

"Michelle, why did you come down here? We were worried sick about you! How long have you known about this secret part of the house? Don't you realize all the trouble and grief you caused?"

"Trouble? ... Grief?" Michelle questioned.

"All I did was fall and landed here! I must have knocked myself out because when I awoke the room was so dark, I couldn't figure out where I was ... Where am I?"

"You mean to tell me you didn't walk down here through all those rooms ?" questioned Tamara.

"I don't know what you're talking about. I wonder if Mom and Dad know there's a cellar way down here," Michelle was still dazed.

"Michelle, listen, I walked through all kinds of rooms to find you. There's a sealed off section of your house. We're standing in it right now. There are also jewels and, and ... Michelle, I saw footprints. If those weren't your footprints someone else must be here ... You don't suppose there's a gho ... ?"

"Nah, don't be silly! Your imagination is working overtime," said Michelle.

"Well, let's get out of here," suggested Tamara.

"What was that?" They simultaneously asked.

A sudden noise forced them to run without looking back.

The house now belongs to the Pennsylvania Historic Society. *'The Never Ending Passage'* is a new tourist attraction. As for Tamara and Michelle, they hope they never see it again.

Pennsylvania's Newest Attraction

Walk Through a 200 Year Old Mansion

with it's Secret Never Ending Passage

Tours Daily from 10:00 a.m. to 4:00 p.m.

Preserved by the
Pennsylvania Historic Society

Jes 'tween Us Two

by Krista Smith
Reisterstown, Maryland
Grade 8, Maryvale

Ben Hampton stood tall and proud. He had strong hands due to years of hard farm work. A man of few words, he was dignified and appeared to be rather serious but with his grandson, Jeff he was anything but serious.

Jeffrey loved his Grandpa Ben. He loved to ride on his shoulders and ask questions about the world and its many creatures. Jeffrey was curious about everything and that was one of the many reasons Grandpa and Jeffrey became so close.

Jeffrey's mother and father were very busy much of the time. They owned a small business. Grandpa Ben always seemed to have time for him. Today Jeffrey was going to be with Grandpa Ben for the whole day. This wasn't going to be an ordinary visit with Grandpa; this day would change his life forever.

"Hello, Jeffrey. How's my buddy?" grandpa asked his grandson.

"Oh, I'm fine, Grandpa... How about you?"

"I'm feelin' good. A beautiful day today, Jeffrey, isn't it?" Grandpa was smiling one of his biggest smiles.

"It sure is, Grandpa," Jeffrey said as he climbed into Grandpa's lap.

"You know, Jeffrey, I think we should take a walk into the woods after we tend the sheep. That was a pretty big storm last night; let's see if there's any damage. What do you say, kiddo?"

"You mean go exploring?" asked Jeffrey with eyes big and bright. Grandpa put his coffee cup in the sink and folded up the morning paper.

"Come on Grandpa Ben, let's hurry." They walked outside with Sadie following close behind. Grandpa Ben didn't go to many places without the collie following.

"Wanna ride on my shoulders?" asked Grandpa.

"Sure," said Jeffrey.

Grandpa Ben sat down on the steps and Ben hopped on.

"You know, Grandpa, I love spending time with you," Jeffrey said hugging his Grandpa around the neck.

"That's because we're best buddies," Grandpa Ben replied. When they arrived at the barn, Grandpa and Jeffrey fed the sheep and gave them fresh water.

"You know, Grandpa, we've never taken the back road through the woods," said Jeffrey looking with hopeful anticipation.

"Well then, today we shall," Grandpa Ben replied. The two of them began walking down the hill toward the narrow path which led into the woods.

"Grandpa, Grandpa, look at the feather."

"Where?" asked Grandpa Ben.

"Up there," Jeffrey said, pointing to a small feather being carried by the wind. "I think I'll catch it so I can make a wish."

Jeffrey's eyes were set on the feather. He began to run as he followed it. Finally it settled on top of a mud puddle. Jeffrey picked up the feather and wiped it on his overalls.

"Can I still make a wish on it, Grandpa, can I?"

"Sure," returned Grandpa, "but you can't tell anyone what you wished for or it won't come true," Grandpa Ben warned.

"It looks like that feather might have belonged to a cardinal," Grandpa continued. He studied the feather with great interest.

"Should I give it back? Maybe he needs it," suggested Jeffrey.

"Well, Jeffrey," said Grandpa, "when I was a boy just about your age, I found a blue jay's feather. I searched for that jay for a long time and finally I found it. Do you know what that blue jay told me? She told me that she didn't need the feather anymore. In fact, she taught me that birds always lose feathers and get new ones to replace them. It happens all the time." Grandpa Ben whispered, "Don't tell anyone 'cause it's jes 'tween us two."

"Okay, Grandpa," Jeffrey replied holding the feather close to him. Grandpa Ben and Jeffrey continued their walk down the path. Grandpa pointed out a brown turtle slowly moving in the grass. Jeffrey walked over and tapped the turtle on its shell. Faster than lightning, the head and legs disappeared.

"Grandpa Ben, why do turtles carry their houses on their backs?"

"Well, Jeff, one day I asked a turtle that very question. He told me that he carried his house around the woods as he looked for meals because it was much easier for him that way. Frankly, I think turtles like to hide when they get scared. You know, the way you hide when it's time for you to get a haircut."

Grandpa Ben looked at Jeffrey with that warm twinkle in his eye. "Don't tell anyone though, 'cause it's jes 'tween us two."

"The stream where we go fishin' is right up here," Grandpa said.

"How will we get across?" Jeffrey asked.

"We'll walk across," Grandpa answered. Carefully they chose large, solid rocks and crossed the stream together. When they got to the bank,

Grandpa picked up a small, flat stone and skillfully skipped it across the stream.

"Grandpa, how did you do that?" Jeffrey asked.

"Magic!" Grandpa Ben replied.

"Do I have magic?" Jeffrey wanted to know.

"Sure you do, but you have your own kind of magic. Everybody does. As you grow it will grow too. You'll find out all kinds of things about yourself and you'll learn to use your magic better and better."

"Really?" asked Jeffrey.

"Really," answered Grandpa.

Jeffrey reached down and picked up a small, pink rock and put it in his pocket for safe keeping. Then he reached up and squeezed Grandpa's hand affectionately, and they walked on. After a few minutes, Jeffrey pulled the rock out of his pocket and re-examined it.

"Grandpa, why are rocks different shapes and colors?"

"You know, Jeff, one day I was asking myself the very same question and so I walked over and sat in front of that big oak tree over there and I thought about it for a very long time. Just when I was leaving to wash up for dinner, I saw a squirrel hunting around for his dinner. I decided to ask him. The squirrel explained that if rocks weren't different colors and shapes, he wouldn't be able to tell the difference between rocks and nuts and that would make it hard for him to find food. But don't tell anyone, Jeff, because this is jes 'tween us two."

Grandpa had so many wonderful tales. He enjoyed telling them as obvious by the delight in his face. Jeffrey also loved the stories and he especially loved these marvelous moments they spent together.

"Grandpa, do you remember telling me about the wise old owl? ... Well, I think you're wiser than he is." Jeffrey leaned against Grandpa and hugged his leg. Quickly, his mood changed.

"Grandpa, why don't animals talk to me?"

"They do, Jeffrey, you just have to listen harder. You have to listen with your eyes, ears and heart. From the time I was your age, whenever I had a question I took a walk through these woods. I always found an answer. You know, animals need us to take care of them but we need them too."

Grandpa's voice was very soft now. "All living creatures must work together."

He stopped and picked up an acorn and held it in the palm of his hand. "See this little acorn, the squirrel plants it and it grows to become a tree."

That night as Jeffrey lay in bed, he thought about the farm, the animals and everything he learned. Mostly, he thought about his Grandpa Ben and the many secrets they shared.

Jeffrey looked out the window at the moon and said, "When I grow up, I want to be just like Grandpa Ben, but don't tell anyone 'cause it's jes 'tween us two."

My Titan Dream Trip

by Patrick Rigby
Hanover, Maryland
Grade 6, St. Augustine

It was Saturday, February 29. My alarm clock had just started to ring. I lay there in bed thinking about what might happen on today's flight. We were heading toward one of Saturn's largest moons, Titan. I am an astronaut.

I got out of bed and started down the hall of bedrooms at NASA. I found Chuck, my co-pilot, laying in bed snoring his head off. I grabbed a pitcher of icy water and poured it on his face.

"Chuck," I exclaimed, "We're late, so get your lazy bones out of that bed."

I went back to my bedroom and started shaving. Next, I got out the clothes I would wear. Finally, I turned on the water for a nice warm shower. I knew this would be the last one I'd have for quite a while.

Thirty minutes later, I got out. I flipped on the TV and the news popped on. I wondered if the newscaster would say anything about the launch today. Almost immediately I heard the news.

"There will be a dangerous launch today to Titan. What it will be like, we don't know. Orbiting satellites report that the terrain is very rocky which may cause considerable problems for landing." I flicked off the TV hoping that I wouldn't encounter Titan's dangerous and rocky terrain.

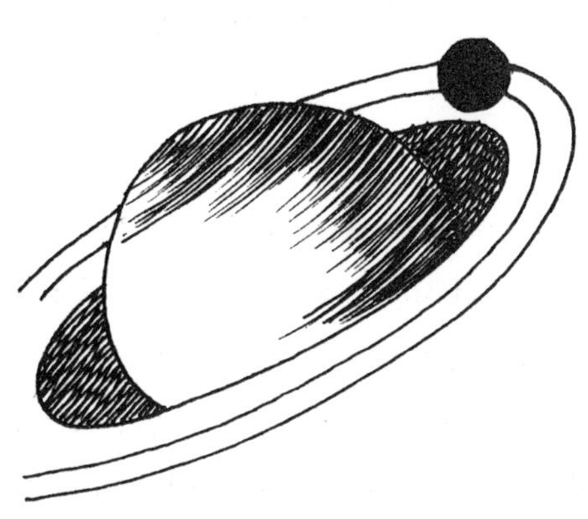

"Chuck, are you ready yet?" I yelled.

"No, not quite. I'm rushing as fast as I can. Wouldn't you know there's no hot water left for my shower!"

I made no comment. By now I was completely dressed and took a dose of medicine for a little cold I had. I went downstairs for breakfast: orange juice, scrambled eggs, bacon and a mug of black coffee.

As I headed back upstairs, Chuck was rushing down. "Calm down, Chuck," I said in passing. I went upstairs to brush my teeth and forgot I had no toothpaste. So, I just rinsed my mouth with water.

I went to the launch pad to meet the engineers and crew. Chuck finally rushed in and we were introduced to Bill, the head engineer. For the next few minutes everyone was wishing us good luck and happy trails. Rob, the flight scientist, finally urged us to get moving because it was almost 11:00 a.m. We were scheduled for a 3:00 p.m. launch and it takes quite a while to get into our flight suits and check everything out.

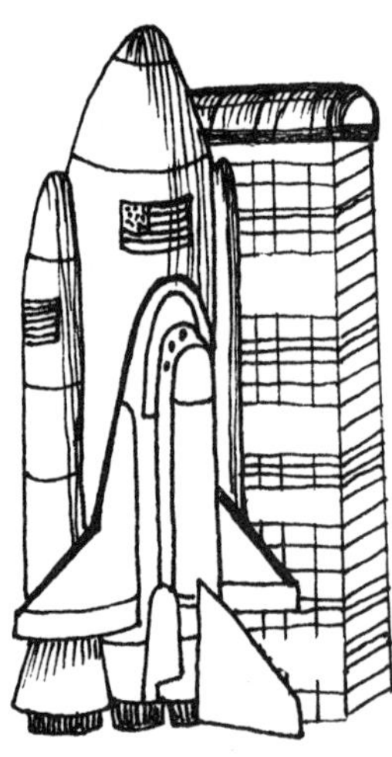

Once suited up, we entered the shuttle. We next went through the pre-flight checklist and everything was moving along rapidly. At 3:00 p.m. we were ready to become the first men to land on Titan. Countdown started: 10, 9, 8, 7, 6, 5, 4, 3, 2, 1. We have lift off! Within 10 minutes, Earth became a tiny speck in space.

At this moment I found myself remembering that at the young age of six, I knew I wanted to be an astronaut. For all these years, I dreamed of flying to the moon of another planet.

Crraaaaash! We felt quite an abrupt impact on Titan's surface. We had hoped for something better. Anxious about the shuttle, we took quick inventory. Fortunately no one was hurt.

Titan was desolate as we expected, but not quite as rocky. It was more like the deserts of earth, dry and somber. Rob tried to taste the air and found it poisonous. Chuck and I then got out of the ship with our helmets and tanks of oxygen. We wanted to communicate with ground control but found our radio in bad condition due to the crash landing.

Suddenly we saw Rob trying to escape in a capsule.

"Grab him," yelled Chuck.

Bill, seeing what was happening at the same time as we, already had hold of him.

"I've got him, Captain," he confirmed.

We didn't know what was going on. We were not even aware of an escape capsule. Rob confessed that the engineers were spies trying to sabotage the flight. They wanted the cosmonauts of Russia to be the first men on Titan. Our rough impact was caused by a planned malfunction in the control board.

We decided that we couldn't trust Rob and so handcuffed him. Using a radio in the capsule, we communicated all that had happened. NASA police quickly picked up the spies in the ground control station. We performed a few of our experiments, gathered some samples of the surface and started the countdown for our return. 10, 9, 8, 7, 6, 5, 4, 3, 2, 1, R-r-i-i-n-g!

"Time to get up for school, Scott," my mother softly called.

"What, what?" I confusingly asked.

"Oh, brother!" I yawned. I knew my Titan dream trip had just ended.

The Fish That Wished to Live on Land

by Tracy Dye
Baltimore, Maryland
Grade 2, Kingsville Elementary

Once upon a time there was a little fish named, Sandy. She wanted to live on land. She had become bored swimming around in the sea. She constantly asked her mother to let her go up on land. Everytime she asked, her mother would lovingly say,

"No, no, Sandy, the sea is best for you."

At night, when everyone else was resting and things were a bit more peaceful, Sandy would think how it would be to live on land.

One day Sandy went to speak with Clarissa Crab.

"Oh, Clarissa," Sandy said. "I need your help."

"Really?" asked Clarissa. "How may I help you?"

"Well," replied Sandy, " I really want to live on land. What should I do?"

"The only way you can do that," said Clarissa Crab,"is to swim way up through the water until you don't see any more fish."

"Oh, thank you," said Sandy, carefully gliding by one of Clarissa's claws.

Sandy began swimming upward, smiling as she went. Up and up and up, she swam. Farther and farther she went, where she saw fewer and fewer fish. Finally on top of the water, she started the last lap toward land. She couldn't wait to show her mother.

On arrival, she was so excited! She wanted to see everything. Very soon, however, she found she couldn't breathe too well. Her body was aching.

Quickly, she threw herself back into the water. Sandy Fish swam down into the sea. She played tag with fish as she swam back to find her mother. This was her home and now she knew what a delightful place it was.

Will My Parents Still Love Me?

by Kathleen Day
Lutherville, Maryland
Grade 8, Maryvale

Maggie, was a loveable little girl who enjoyed the attention her parents constantly gave her. She never knew what it was to wait for anything, for she was an only child. She liked playing with Mom and Dad and they liked playing games with her too. Maggie was very bright and so her Mom and Dad spoke to her about all kinds of interesting things.

One day at dinner they said to her, "Maggie, guess what? We're going to have a baby and you will have a little sister or brother to play with. Isn't that exciting?"

Maggie began to imagine what that would mean. She didn't think she was going to like this. The more she thought, the worse she felt. Finally, anger and confusion began welling up in her. She stomped out of the kitchen, up the stairs and into her bedroom. She slammed the door as hard as she could.

Maggie sat in her room for what seemed to be hours. She cried and thought about all the attention the new baby would take from her. Maggie decided to run away and get her parents really worried. She thought that perhaps her parents might change their minds about a new baby.

"Then," she reasoned, "they would only take care of me, the way they always do."

Her parents tried again to speak to her about the new baby during the nightly bedtime routine. Maggie would not listen. She kept changing the subject.

After her parents lovingly tucked her in and said good night, she planned what she would do next. Quietly, Maggie gathered some things together. She took a book of nursery rhymes, Garfield slippers and the teddy bear, named Pooky. She sneaked out the back door and up into the tree house which Daddy had built for her. Spreading the Barbie sleeping bag on the floor boards, she fell asleep.

The next morning Maggie was awakened by a loud scream which was probably her mother walking into an empty bedroom. She peered out of the treehouse window trying to see the activity inside her own home. Both of her parents were frantically turning the house inside out looking for her. They ran from room to room calling her name. Then she saw her father race out to the car and drive through the neighborhood in search of her. Her mother got on the phone and was calling everyone to learn Maggie's whereabouts. Maggie continued watching from her hiding place.

Maggie was getting tired of being up in the tree house alone. She missed her parents. She was just about to climb down, when she saw her father return. His face was sad and distressed. Maggie felt sorry for him and wanted to rush down and kiss him but she just couldn't. She only watched and felt awful inside.

Finally hungry, bored and feeling sick, Maggie decided to go home. She climbed down from the tree house and opened the back door. No one heard her or saw her go up to her room. She tried to play with her toys. Hunger forced her downstairs for something to eat. She pulled from the refrigerator all her favorite foods: pickles, mayonnaise, ketchup, turkey, olives and ham. From the pantry, she got potato chips, marshmallows, cereal, and chocolate chip cookies. She put a little bit of everything between some bread and then took her lunch upstairs.

Her mother, returning from another frantic search in the neighborhood, walked into the kitchen. Once she saw the mess, she knew that either Maggie was close by or somehow raccoons had invaded the house. Maggie's mother raced the stairs and grabbed Maggie up into her arms.

"Oh, Maggie," she cried, "don't ever do that again. Your father and I were so worried. Where were you? Why did you do that?" Her words kept tumbling out. She kept holding onto Maggie. Maggie started crying. She felt awful.

Finally Maggie admitted, "I thought you didn't love me any more."

Maggie knew she was being selfish. She also admitted that she was afraid to share her parents' love with a brother or sister. She quietly said, "I thought you wouldn't pay attention to me with a new baby around. I ... I ... ran away so you would miss me." She started sobbing.

Maggie and her Mom stood there holding onto each other, both of them were crying as they tried to give comfort to the other. Finally, Maggie's Mom was able to talk again.

"Honey, I would never ignore you or forget about you. You are my first baby, ... my dear, precious, daughter. No matter how many children we have in our family, Dad and I will always love you."

Still Standing

by Maggie Litz
White Hall, Maryland
Grade 8, Maryvale

"Sometimes I still cry at night."

"Why, Grandma?"

"Oh, just because I miss her."

"Miss who, Grandma?"

"Lacey."

"Lacey?...Who's Lacey?"

"You mean I haven't told you about Lacey? Gee, I can't imagine that. Come here, Ali, and sit on my lap. I'll tell you all about Lacey."

Grandma cleared her throat and then began.

"Let's see, now. Where shall I start? Well, Lacey had long, flowing brown hair and beautiful green eyes, ... eyes like I'd never seen before or since." Grandma began to smile as she remembered.

"You know, I think I need to go back even further

than that."

Grandma began again.

When I was a young girl, I was very lonely. In our neighborhood there weren't too many children my age. There was only one girl and naturally we became very good friends. We did everything together. Then one day, a big yellow truck drove up to her house. I went over to see what was happening and found out a moving van was taking my friend to California.

I was so upset. I stayed in my room for a week just crying and feeling sorry for myself. When I finally came out, Mother decided to send me to Ohio to visit Aunt Linda. She thought a change would do me good. Perhaps I'd stay the whole summer, but she'd decide that later. Well, it was in Ohio that I met Lacey.

Grandmother entered into the story as if it were happening all over again.

I got off the plane and was greeted warmly by Aunt Linda. She ran up to me and surrounded me with her warm hug. As she cupped my shoulder with her arm, we walked together through the airport.

"I'm so glad you came. Were you scared to come all that way on a plane by yourself? Well, let's get you home and settled in."

We went to the baggage claim, got my bags and waited at the curb for a taxi. It was different in Ohio. People greeted you easily with, 'Hi' or 'Have a nice day.' Nobody did that in Denver unless they knew you. In no time at all a bright, yellow taxi pulled up and asked, "Where to?"

Aunt Linda replied, "1632 West Jersey Street," and we were on our way.

It was a hot sticky day in Ohio, unlike any in Denver. I was beginning to feel a bit homesick but thought if my cousin, Sara is there everything will be okay.

"Aunt Linda, is Sara home?"

"No, I'm sorry, honey, she's away at camp."

"When will she be back?"

"Oh honey, she'll be gone for a month. You see we had made plans before your mother called. ... I'm sorry. We wouldn't have, had we known. ..."

Heaving a sigh, I meekly said, "Oh."

"Don't worry, Sweetie, we'll have lots of fun together," Aunt Linda said with another hug around my shoulders. For the next twenty minutes or so there was silence and then we arrived at 1632 West Jersey Street. Aunt Linda's house was a grayish-white, single home, quite beautiful. The cabbie got my bags. Aunt Linda gave him some money and there we were.

"This is your new home for a while. How do you like it?"

"I like it a lot. It's lovely," I politely answered.

"We like it too. It cost a pretty penny but it's sure worth it."

"I guess it is," I said trying to sound interested.

"Okay now, let's get you settled upstairs."

Aunt Linda pushed the front door which opened with a slight creak. It revealed a spacious foyer, a sitting room and large living room. The stairs, covered with an oriental rug were to the right of the foyer. Aunt Linda led the way to the second floor bedroom which would be mine. Around the corner, down the hall to the second room on the left, and we were there. To my surprise, the room was rather small but cozy. There was a bed, desk, chair and a large wooden dresser.

"Put your clothes away and then come down for lunch, okay."

I picked up my bags and put them on the bed to unpack. I felt a cool breeze and looked up. The window over the desk was open behind a flapping pink curtain. I pulled the curtain back so to enjoy more sunlight. Now the room looked happier. Glancing out the window, I noticed a small forest not too far from the house. I made a mental note and then started unpacking.

After I was finished, I went downstairs to have lunch. I didn't have any trouble finding the kitchen. My nose led the way. I was starved. Aunt Linda had left a plate with a hot turkey sandwich on it and a glass of milk. As I shoved down the sandwich, I picked up a note leaning against my glass.

Meaghan,

So sorry to run out on you already but there was an emergency at the school. Eat your lunch and relax, I'll be back within the hour.

Love,
Aunt Linda

P.S. There's a store just across the street. Could you please pick up some milk? Thanks so much. I left the money on the fridge. Thanks again.

After I finished eating, I picked up the money and put it in my pocket. It was still rather warm outside. The sun was bright and there was a warm breeze. I found the store easily and got the milk.

I walked quickly back to the house intending to explore it. I walked up the few steps to the front door, turned the knob and pushed. The door didn't budge. I pushed again. No use, I was locked out. I didn't have a key so I put the milk on the steps and decided to look more closely at the young forest.

No longer walking, the wind forced me into a tiny trot. Eagerly I entered on the small path. Everything was green and plush. A tree in the distance looked bigger and wider than all the others. It caught and held my eye. The bark was chestnut brown and the leaves deep green. I was compelled to make my way to the tree.

"I'm so glad you came," I heard a voice saying. "I've been pruning ever since I knew you were coming." I turned around in the direction of the voice and there was a young girl about my age, standing there. She had long brown hair and brilliant green eyes.

"Hi, my name is Lacey; what's yours?"

"I'm Meaghan," I found myself answering.

"Hi, Meaghan, it's nice to finally meet you."

"How did you know I was coming?" I asked.

"My friend, Krysta from Denver, sent me a brief message telling me you were coming for the summer. I'm awfully glad you came," she added. "As you see there aren't too many people who live around here."

"Well, it's nice to meet you too," I replied. "Do you live near here?"

"I do," was all she answered. Then she asked, "Where do you live?"

"I'm staying with my Aunt Linda in the big grayish-white house over there." I pointed to the house because you could still see part of it from where we stood.

"I love that house. I always wondered what it was like inside," said Lacey.

"Come on over, I'll show you around when Aunt Linda comes back."

"Oh, no, I couldn't," Lacey protested.

"Sure, you could," I objected.

"No, maybe some other time." Changing the subject, she asked, "There's a small but lovely stream nearby, would you like to see it?"

Lacey began walking but I thought I that I should get back to Aunt Linda's. We made plans to meet tomorrow.

When I got back, Aunt Linda was pacing up and down the sidewalk by the house. She looked worried and upset. I decided not to bug her by telling her about the locked door or my new friend.

"How did it go," I inquired of her emergency meeting.

"Not too well. I'm so sorry about all this. I am utterly exhausted now," she said. "I don't feel up to much more today. All I want is some rest."

"That's okay, I'm tired myself."

"When I wake up, I'll fix you some dinner. Sound good?" Aunt Linda asked.

"Sounds good," I replied.

I walked into the house, up to my room and fell sound asleep. I awakened with an aroma of bacon and eggs in the house. I hopped out of bed and went downstairs. Laid out on the counter were eggs,a plate full of bacon, toast and pancakes, milk and orange juice. I realized that I had slept through dinner and it was now breakfast time. Aunt Linda was nowhere around but without looking much, I spotted another note.

> *Meaghan,*
>
> *Sorry again to run out on you but they needed my help at the school. I left some breakfast and there's plenty of food in the fridge for lunch. There's also a key hanging by the door. Take it along if you go anywhere, so you don't get locked out. I should be home before dinner. Why don't you have some fun exploring our quaint neighborhood?*
>
> *Love,*
> *Aunt Linda*

Breakfast was a little cold but still good. After I finished washing my dishes, I went upstairs to get dressed. I couldn't wait to see Lacey again. I put on some jeans and a blue shirt and ran out the door with the key in my hand. It wasn't as hot as yesterday but still warm. I walked over to the forest looking for Lacey.

"Lacey, Lacey," I called. "Where are you?"

"Hi, Meaghan, you came!" She walked out from behind one of the trees. "Do you want to see the stream today?"

"Sure, let's go."

"We won't take long; it's not far. We'll be gone just a minute or two, I promise."

For a second, I thought she was talking to the trees. "No, that's crazy," I thought again.

The stream was actually the loveliest I had ever seen. It had a winding bed of crystal clear water. You could see colored stones as well as tiny fish floating near the bottom. I took my shoes off, placed them near a tree and walked in. It was cool but refreshing.

"What a wonderful forest," I said to her.

"It is wonderful, isn't it? You can find everything important here."

"What do you mean?" I asked.

"Well, I guess it's time I told you," said Lacey.

"Told me what?"

"About myself," she hesitated and then said "Oh Augusta, where do I start?"

"Augusta? ... Who's Augusta? What is going on here and what are you talking about?" I was feeling completely confused.

"Meaghan, it's a long story. My name is Lacilia Amarada Sade. They call me Lacey for short.

"Who calls you Lacey?"

"Well, the treemenites and the trees do," offered Lacey.

"The what? Is this some kind of wild imagination you've got or..."

Lacey interrupted her. "Meaghan, I'm a treemenite. The girl Krysta I told you about is a treemenite too. We have a special mission to protect trees. It seems no one else will. Too many people are clearing away the trees. Augusta, the tree guardian of the earth, sent some of us into the forests to protect them. One way we do that is to help young people learn about the danger."

I interrupted this time. "Lacey, this is too incredible!"

"Oh, Meaghan, listen, please. Our environment is being destroyed. No one wants to face the problem and deal with it. You can help Meaghan. You know that every time a tree is cut down there is less oxygen in the air. The atmosphere is thinning out and its getting dirty. With all the pollution going on, we need more trees, not fewer."

"You're serious, aren't you? ... Are there, uh, treemenites all around us? What happens if a tree does get cut down? Does it hurt the treemenite?"

"There is a treemenite for every tree. When a tree is cut down, Augusta sends the treemenite back to Naples for more training. It's her way to teach us how to keep guard and to protect the trees."

"How come I can't see these other treemenites but can see you?" I asked.

"A treemenite is only allowed to be seen by one person. You're the person I chose to see me."

I walked over to a nearby tree. "What's the name of the treemenite for this tree?" I asked.

"I think it's Galley."

"Tell her I said, 'hi.'" I looked around as I spoke to see if I might find her.

"She says, 'hi' to you too. Meaghan, I think we should get back."

Lacey started to run.

"Lacey, Lacey, why are you running? Wait up." I was panting and running and trying to make sense out of all this.

"I have a feeling something terrible has happened," Lacey yelled over her shoulder.

"What Lacey, what?" I called.

When I reached the end of the path, I saw her tragedy. A construction worker had just cut down six trees; one of them was Lacey's. She was huddled down by the tree stump looking like her heart was broken. I ran over to her and tried to comfort her.

"I'm so sorry," I said. I knew what was going to happen next.

"I have to go now," she whispered. "Augusta is calling me. Meaghan, before I go promise me that you will not forget me and that you will do what you can to save the trees and yourself."

"Lacey, don't go," I pleaded. "Please come back." But, I knew she couldn't. I didn't know what to do so I started running. I just ran and ran not knowing where I was going or what I was doing. Finally, I figured out what I had to do. I had to plant trees for the six that were just cut down. I knew it wasn't enough but I felt it was something.

"Oh, Grandma, and did you plant trees?" asked young Ali.

"I did. Come I'll show you. Here are the six I planted and they're still standing."

"This one is especially beautiful, Grandma." Ali pointed to the tallest and strongest of the trees.

"Yes, that one I chose especially for Lacey."

"Oh, Grandma, do you think Lacey is here?" asked Ali.

"I don't know Ali, maybe."

"I'm here Meaghan. Thank you for the beautiful tree. You haven't visited Ohio since I left you there, so long ago. Thanks for remembering. I love you, Meaghan."

Lacey's words were whispers which only the other trees and treemenites could hear.

Cat Alert

by Pimpila Thanaporn
Baltimore, Maryland
Grade 8, Maryvale

After everyone is in bed and all is quiet, the kitchen appliances of the Thompson household come to life. No one knows this secret but the family cat and she doesn't like it. One night was filled with more adventure than usual.

"Rrrrr, Rrrrr," whirred Billy Blender. "Hurry, wake up!"

Hearing all the noise, Mrs. Spoon got out of bed. "What's all the fuss?" she asked.

Billy pointed to the cat creeping their way. "Cat alert!" he signaled.

Hearing the alarm, everyone woke up. They had practiced cat drills before and knew exactly what to do. Chris Cookie Jar led the way to the children's playroom. They dressed in doll's clothing to disguise themselves and then sat behind the other toys. Just as the cat walked in, their luck ran out. Mrs. Spoon, still speckled with pepper, let out a powerful sneeze "Aa-aa-choo." She had blown their cover! The kitchen crew now ran for the door. Too late, the cat was blocking the door with his furry body and powerful claws.

Billy Blender tried whirling past but he used the wrong speed. Too slow to get past the cat, Rhonda Rolling Pin raced into action. She rolled over the cat's tail leaving him unable to stretch out his paw far enough to scratch Billy.

"Me-e-o-o-ow," screeched the cat.

Now he was really angry; time to try another escape. Racing to the bathroom, the appliances quickly slammed the door behind them. They had never seen the bathroom before. For the moment, the cat was forgotten as they saw their reflections in the large mirror. Other shiny fixtures gave off their reflections too. They wanted a better look. How could they climb up higher? Mrs. Spoon pointed to the roll of toilet tissue.

"That's the way up," she said. With every effort to climb up, the toilet roll turned and down they fell only to be covered by the unraveling paper. Sally Spoon even fell into the waste basket.

"Help, help," she cried. Her loud cries awakened Tommy Toothbrush.

"What's the trouble?" he asked.

"My baby has fallen into the waste basket," wailed Mrs. Spoon.

"Don't worry," said Tommy Toothbrush. "I'll get her out." He jumped down from his perch on the sink and leaned on his bristles. Then carefully balancing himself on the edge of the waste basket, he called down to Sally.

"Can you hear me?" he asked.

"Yes," she timidly replied.

"I'm going to hang on with my bristles and you grab hold of my long, lean body. Are you ready? Here I come."

Sally Spoon was out in no time and Mrs. Spoon couldn't thank Tommy enough. For his bravery and daring the appliances applauded, agreeing that he was certainly the hero of the house.

Now to get back to the kitchen was their next big feat. Trying to tiptoe down the hall, they were just about to enter the kitchen when someone warned, *Cat alert!* They raced across the floor with the cat close behind them. Suzy Sink waited for the perfect moment. She sprayed freezing cold water on the cat below. Needless to say, the cat left in a hurry and the appliances were safe with their secret for one more time.

Next morning, the Thompsons felt completely stumped as they tried to figure how water was splashed all over the kitchen floor.

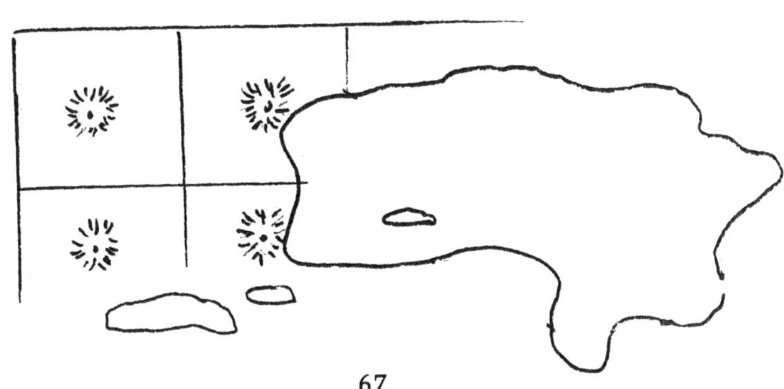

The Intruder

by Eric Seebach
Baltimore, Maryland
Grade 9, Chesapeake High School

"Bye, Mom and Dad," I excitedly screamed from my room. My parents were leaving for an overnight business meeting at the luxurious Hyatt Regency Hotel at the Inner Harbor in downtown Baltimore.

I now had the whole house to myself. My first mischievous thought was to party. My mind raced like a cheetah; food, soda, who to call and all the rest. But after a few insane minutes, I decided that I couldn't let my trusting parents down. They let me stay at home instead of leaving me with the boring, Miss Frankfort.

So, I ran down the stairs to our country kitchen and raided the refrigerator. I was soon sitting in my room with my Super Nintendo controller playing, *Street Fighter II*. I gulped down the delicious, turkey club sandwich, thinking how good it was. Maybe I should become a gourmet chef, I chuckled to myself.

Everything was perfect. There was a bright, full moon among shining stars. I was playing superbly. In fact, I was killing the hardest character, M. Bison with the game's fireball, when I heard a loud crash downstairs. I flicked off the Nintendo thinking I would never in my whole life get that far in the game.

The crash was soon followed by other noises. My heart thumped like a hammer against a steel nail as I heard plodding footsteps stalking around downstairs.

"Oh, my God," I thought, filled with panic, "A burglar!" I grabbed my Louisville Slugger and switched off the lights. Then slowly and quietly, I crawled under my bed. My heart was now pounding like a jackhammer as I heard the figure downstairs plunder our precious belongings.

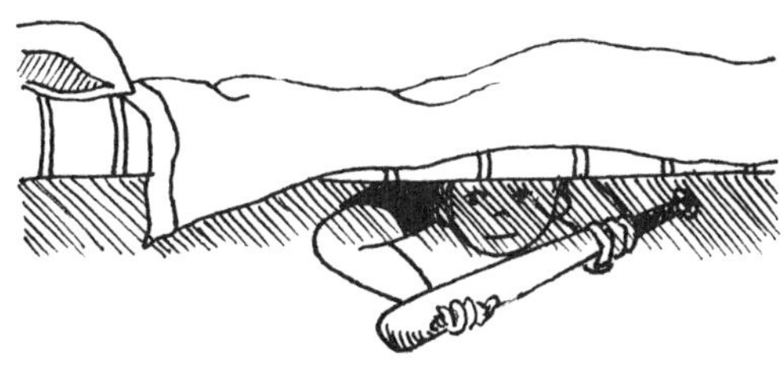

"What should I do?" I could feel panic. I couldn't call the police because the burglar would hear me.

"What if he has a gun? Oh, God, don't let him come up here." As if he read my thoughts, the burglar's flashlight shone at the top of the stairs. I could hear him creep up our newly carpeted stairs. The painstakingly quiet house was magnifying each new footstep.

Then, all of a sudden, something was under the bed with me. I felt a fuzzy thing rub across my face.

"Oh, no, Spuds!" I screamed inside my mind. "Why on earth is he here now?" Spuds was a tabby cat from the house next door who always found a way to sneak into our house and torment me. Somehow I think he knows I'm allergic to cats! Spuds started purring close to my face and I was nearly choking and trying not to sneeze.

The figure was now at the top of the stairs. I could tell it was a man about six feet tall and somewhat overweight from the shadow cast into the hallway. He tiptoed into our bathroom and I heard his heavy breathing as he looked around in the shower stall.

Spuds was really purring a lot at this point and I was holding my breath to keep from reacting. The intruder was making his way into my parent's room. I heard him stumbling around in the room next to mine as he looked in my parent's closets. As the burglar closed a closet door, I slithered out from under the bed and stood next to my doorway with the baseball bat in my hand.

"This is it," I thought. "I'll only get one shot at him. I have to plant this right on his head."

My heart stopped as I saw the beam of light from his flashlight shine in front of my doorway. I saw one foot advance the threshold into my room. I swung the bat like the mighty Casey and like the mighty Casey, I struck out. At the same moment as I swung the bat, the man stooped down to scoop up Spuds.

"Spuds," he said to the darting cat. "Here you are." It was the voice of Jim our neighbor.

"Mr. Jim," I said in a shaking voice.

"Eric," he responded equally surprised, as I flipped on the lights.

"What are you doing here?" he asked.

"More importantly, what are YOU doing here?" I demanded.

"Since I have an extra key to your house, I thought I'd check to see if Spuds was here. I thought you guys went out."

"My parents did," I said. "What did you break downstairs?"

"Oh, after I opened the door, I bumped into the lamp trying to find the light switch. Then, I had to find a flashlight..." I cut him off.

"Well, you can leave now," I said a little perturbed.

"Sure, Eric, I'm really sorry about..."

"Good night, Mr. Jim," I replied, not being too patient nor too polite.

So, he took his cat and left me alone with my Louisville Slugger and my annoyance that I had to turn off my Nintendo game for this?!!!

Door to Discovery

by Katherine A. Malloy
Ellicott City, Maryland
Grade 10, Mount de Sales Academy

"Mom, have you seen my purple shirt?" asked Andrea McPhearson.

"I think it's in box 2B, dear," replied her mother.

"O K, Mom," said Andrea as she returned to her unpacking. "Transfer, a stupid transfer," she muttered. Her father's job had moved and consequently, so had her family. They had just gotten to their new house yesterday. Andrea had been constantly grumpy since her mother started packing for the move.

As Andrea rummaged through the box, her brother came into her room. He was playing his Game Boy, until someone unpacked and hooked up the Nintendo.

"What's up?" he asked.

"More unpacking, Shawn," she replied. "What else! I can't believe that Mom and Dad think we can just move like this! I mean it's..."

Shawn just tuned her out. This has been Andrea's favorite subject since the moving van pulled into the driveway the day before.

"And I had to leave my friends, and my school and..."

"School hasn't started yet, Dria," replied Shawn. "You'll make new friends. The kids in this neighborhood seem pretty cool."

"Great," Andrea said sarcastically. "I'm being advised by a nine-year-old on how to continue my life. Sure, the boys your age seem fine, but I think the girls are stuck up."

"Mom says you've been horribly negative about this move," replied Shawn. "Your making it harder on everyone. I think you have an attitude problem, Dria."

"Go away," replied Andrea. Shawn left. Andrea turned and looked in her mirror. She ran her fingers through her short, wavy, blond hair.

"Have I really been that awful? No," she decided. "It's not my fault. I didn't ask to move."

In her heart, she knew that she was adding to everyone's difficulty. Andrea returned to her unpacking. As she reached up to place her winter scarf and mittens on the shelf at the top of the closet, she noticed a small door in the closed ceiling. She wondered about it.

"Mom," she called to her mother. "What's the door in the ceiling of my closet for?"

Mrs. McPhearson stuck her head in briefly.

"Probably the way to the attic," she concluded.

"Can I go up there?" asked Andrea.

"Now, in the middle of unpacking? What do you want to go up there for?"

"I just want to see what it looks like," explained Andrea. "Please?"

"All right," agreed her mother. "Just be careful!"

Ever since she was little, she liked to explore. She had been the kid in the neighborhood who climbed the highest, ran the farthest, and swam the deepest. She had discovered many new and interesting things. Maybe the previous owners had left some things of interest behind; she had to find out.

Andrea climbed up onto a ladder and started to push against the door. It was much heavier to push than she expected. Once opened, there was light coming through. She took a deep breath finishing the climb. What a surprise! Andrea expected to see a dusty attic. Instead she found herself in a beautiful, green meadow.

"It must be a dream," she said. "This isn't making any sense." She pinched herself for a reality check. When the meadow didn't disappear she concluded that it had to be real. She peered down through the door to her closet below and saw the clothes and boxes.

"Okay, so this isn't a dream," Andrea said to herself. "What now?"

She looked around. It was a beautiful place. There were pink, purple and yellow flowers growing in the soft green grass. The sky was a sparkling shade of blue with a few clouds in it. A soft breeze flounced her hair.

Andrea shut the door to her closet. It was ingeniously covered with grass so that it blended in with the rest of the meadow. A few strands of bent over grass served as the handle. Andrea removed the red bandana she was wearing and tied it around the handle to find the door again.

Now that she was sure of getting back, Andrea began to walk toward a cluster of hills at the west end of the field. Moving closer, she noticed something strange. It looked like a giant bird. No, it wasn't that at all. It was ... a person with wings? The winged person noticed Andrea too, because at that moment it began to flap its wings and took off.

Andrea was frightened. What if this strange creature was dangerous? Did it eat people?

The winged creature flew closer and closer until Andrea could see that it was a girl about her age. She had long, red hair and wore green clothing made of gauze. The wings, made of green feathers shimmered and changed colors with the light. The wings weren't naturally hers. They were attached to her arms with sleeves.

"Hello," the girl called. "Watch out! I'm going to land."

Andrea got out of the way as the strange girl soared down to where she stood. The girl let the wings fall to her sides.

"Greetings," said the girl. "I'm Lydia Brightsky, amateur aviator. Who are you?"

"I'm... I'm Andrea McPhearson," Andrea replied.

"Hi, Andrea, will you help me with these wings? They're a pain in the neck to get on and off."

Andrea regarded Lydia a little curiously, but helped Lydia pull her arms out of the winged sleeves. Lydia stretched and flexed her arms.

"Much better, thanks," she said. "I can tell you're new here, otherwise, you would know about my brother."

"Your brother?" asked Andrea.

"He's an inventor," Lydia replied. "He built these wings. He invents all sorts of stuff. I don't know what he's working on now." She paused for a few minutes then continued with, "Tell me about yourself."

Andrea was a bit startled by Lydia's abrupt change in subject.

"Well," she began, "I just moved into the neighborhood a few days ago. I was unpacking when I noticed the door in the ceiling of my closet. I thought it went to the attic but instead it came up here.

"Oh, you're from another world," Lydia stated with interest. "What's it like there?"

"Not good," said Andrea. She launched into her monologue about how miserable she has been since her family moved.

Lydia interrupted, "Wouldn't it be better if you tried making new friends? At least, it makes sense to try. Is it your parents' fault they had to move?" she continued.

Then she caught sight of Andrea's angry look. "I'm sorry'" she said. "Did I start preaching to you? I'm forever giving people advice and sometimes they get mad at me."

"Well, it's not that I'm angry, exactly. My brother, Shawn said pretty much the same thing. It's just that ... I know I'm making things worse, but somehow I can't help it ... Not yet, anyway!"

"Andrea, not many people like to admit they're wrong, and certainly not quickly."

"That's true. Thanks, you make me feel better."

Andrea was the one to change the subject abruptly this time as she looked back down at the ground.

"This is a pretty unrealistic thing, being here and all."

"You're right," Lydia said with a grin. "If I came through my closet and saw a girl flying, I would find it pretty unrealistic too."

"But, since I'm here, what's next?" asked Andrea.

"Flying," answered Lydia. It relieves stress, lowers your blood pressure and gives you a deep sense of satisfaction." She laughed at herself then and said, "Not only am I an advice-giver but I think I'm a good sales person too."

"You sold me!" Andrea laughed. "You make it sound great and watching you looks fun; but is it dangerous?"

"Not at all," answered Lydia.

"You know, I had this feeling you'd want to fly. You just look like someone who likes to try new things."

Lydia pointed to a nearby hill. "You can try take off from over there."

Carrying the wings, the two girls walked over towards the hill. Once there Lydia this time, did the helping. After careful adjustments, she instructed Andrea to flap her wings in order to generate power. Then she explained that in the air, she could catch a current and glide. To land, Andrea had to slowly lower her wings. Andrea found it was easier done than said. Within seconds, she was airborne and free.

"I could fly forever," she yelled down to her teacher.

She swooped and dove and then turned.

"You're a natural," Lydia called back to her.

Andrea spotted her red bandana, her own clever door marker. She gently lowered her arms and the wings glided her to the ground.

"I've got to go," she said pointing to her watch.

Lydia nodded. "I understand. Come back to see me some time or maybe I'll ..."

She didn't finish her sentence. She just smiled and waved as Andrea untied her bandana from the handle and opened the door.

"Good-bye, Lydia. It was wonderful."

"Good-bye, Andrea, see you later," said Lydia.

Andrea climbed through her door and found herself in the closet again. The door closed from above. "Lydia must have shut it," she thought.

Mrs. McPhearson came into the bedroom just then. "Was the attic interesting?" she questioned.

"Oh, as interesting as attics get," replied Andrea.

In a few days school started. Andrea timidly entered her homeroom. She took an empty seat in the back row. A few minutes later a girl came into the room saying to the teacher,

"I'm sorry I'm late. There was a mix-up in my records."

Andrea's jaw dropped. The girl may have been wearing jeans and a tee shirt instead of green gauze, but this was definitely Lydia Brightsky.

Lydia walked to the back of the room and sat next to Andrea.

"What are you doing here?" whispered Andrea.

"We're both the kind of people who like to try new things," explained Lydia. "Do you want to come over to my place after school?"

"Sure, why not?" smiled Andrea.

Saving the Bay

by Jamie Lynne Kennedy
Chesapeake Beach, Maryland
Grade 5, Beach Elementary School

"How could they?" Marvin Minnow sat down on an old tin can.

"How could they be so unreliable?"

Marvin Minnow was talking to himself about how dirty the bay had become. It used to be such a beautiful place to live, but now people polluted it making it as dirty as a garbage can.

Just then, Carl Crab crawled by tangled up in a mass of plastic.

"Marvin, whew ... I thought I wasn't going to find anybody. Can you help me out of this mess?"

"What happened to you?" asked Marvin.

"All I was doing was walking along my usual path looking for my breakfast, when right in my path was a trespasser.

"Well," he blushed, "It turned out to be this bunch of plastic. How was I supposed to know? A crab's got to do what a crab's got to do. So, I ... uh ... attacked it."

"Well, it's certainly not your fault," Marvin said, as he swam in and out trying to untangle Carl. "I mean people shouldn't be throwing all this debris in here. The bay is our home."

With some success, he then said to Carl, "Come on. I've had enough of this. Let's get some of our friends together and try to figure out what we can do about this problem."

A half hour later, friends were hovering around Marvin, who was swimming near an old rotten shoe. He started yelling over the commotion, "Thanks for coming, everybody. We've got to see what we can do about ... "

CRASH! The big thud was trash hitting the water. It surrounded them. They tried to break through the filth.

Rita Rockfish sputtered, "They ... they're up there throwing garbage in the bay. I think that boat just dumped it's trash. Look, an old gasoline can, a bottle, candy wrappers, soda cans and a tire. Thank goodness that didn't hit any of us on the head."

"We have to do something," Sammy Sea Turtle exclaimed. "We just can't live in this stuff! Does anyone have any ideas?"

"Hmmmmmmmmm!" Everyone was thinking.

Seymoure Shrimp shouted, "I've got it. We'll go somewhere else!"

Bobby Bluefish, looking sad, replied, "I know it sounds like a good idea but it won't solve anything for the rest of the bay inhabitants, nor for the humans. We just can't swim away from our problems."

"You're right," Seymoure agreed.

Toby Trout said, "We've got to get the people to know that what they're doing is hurting us and them."

"How do you do that?" they commented to each other.

"I don't know," admitted Toby.

"Don't worry," Rita Rockfish said, "We'll find a way. Right now, though, I think everyone should go home and get some rest. Later, after we've rested and did some thinking on our own, we might have some answers."

Marvin Minnow, Carl Crab, Rita Rockfish, Sammy Sea Turtle, Seymoure Shrimp, Bobby Bluefish and Toby Trout all went to their not-so-clean-any-more homes to get some rest. The next morning everyone but Toby was there at the meeting place.

"Does anyone know where Toby is?" Sammy asked.

"Not me."

"Nope."

"Uh, Uh."

"Haven't seen him."

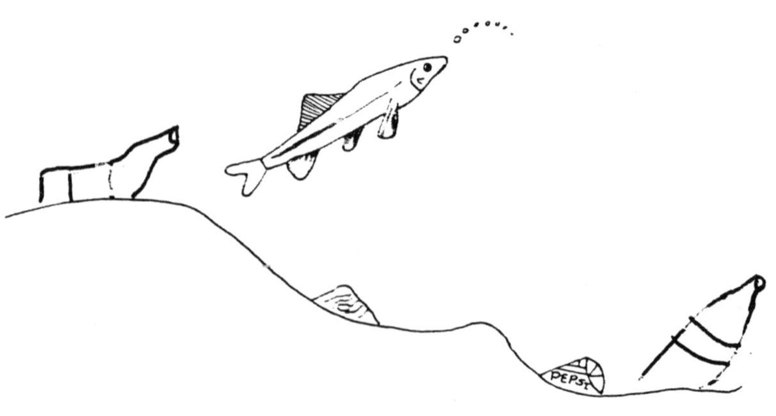

"I wonder where he is?" Sammy said with a puzzled expression. Everyone was getting worried and so the meeting was rather unproductive. A half hour later, Toby came swimming up to them.

"My dear water friends, I think I've got it."

"What is it?" They all wanted to know.

"Well, remember how we were thinking that people needed to know what they were doing? My idea is to show them how the bay is supposed to be. The comparison may help them see the problem. We should start cleaning up the bay ourselves."

"What? You mean all by ourselves?"

"Yeah," replied Toby.

"Do you really think we could pull it off?" questioned Carl.

"Well, sure we could," Toby said. "At least we could try."

"Well, okay, I'll try," said Rita. The others agreed too.

"But I forgot one thing," said Toby. "We'll be in hiding. I think that's important, so that what we're doing won't be figured out until we're done."

"Good idea," Bobby replied. "So, when are we starting?"

"As soon as everyone is ready," said Toby, "we can't let the bay get any worse." So all the excited sea animals went home to get ready. The next day the seven friends were standing together, suitcases in hand, waiting for Toby.

"Where is he?" Sammy asked.

"I don't know," Carl said. "He just told me he'd be a couple minutes late."

In a few minutes, Toby was swimming toward his bay friends.

"Hi, friends, I stopped for some paper and pencils so we could record how much trash we collect each day."

"Good thinking," Bobby Bluefish said.

"Well, let's start off," said Toby happily.

"Where to?" Seymoure inquired.

"You'll see when we get there," said Toby.

"Is it far?" Sammy asked.

"Not far," answered Toby, "It will only take a half hour." Then he laughed and in a teasing manner said,

"Enough with the questions, if everyone has their stuff, let's go."

In exactly one half hour they reached their destination. "We're here."

They swam into an old crab pot. Carl Crab looked at it anxiously. "Where did you find this?"

"One day, I was exploring over by the pier when I came across it. A friendly horseshoe crab was strong enough to move it here for me. It's big enough for all of us and since we may be here for a while, make yourselves at home."

They all settled in and then Toby got them down to business. Rita and Seymoure will work on paper and they also are doing the recording. Marvin and Sammy are going to take care of the plastic. Bobby and Carl have the job of cleaning up cans and Toby had decided to take care of the odd stuff, including glass and metal. After collecting all they could, the plan was to send a letter to humans asking them to pick up the collected trash and recycle it. Toby had more to explain but they were all so anxious to save the bay, that they didn't wait to hear it.

A week later the hard work of the sea animals was showing. The bay looked better than it had for a long time. Sara Seagull acted as courier. The letter explaining what they had done, where the trash was stored, and how to help was soon on its way. Luckily, Sara delivered the letter to a caring and conscientious person. Toby's plan worked.

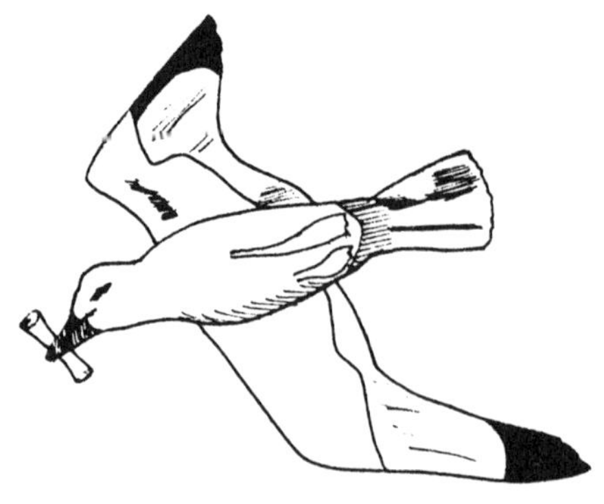

The bay creatures still keep an eye on the bay but now the humans have been alerted to their responsibilities.

(llustrations by Jamie Lynn Kennedy)

The Perfect V

by Jennifer Gray
Parkton, Maryland
Grade 8, Maryvale

Mother Duck had been nesting in the marsh for at least three weeks. On one beautiful spring day, five little ducklings hatched and popped their heads out to greet her. Their first feelings were for rest, after such a strenuous struggle to crack their shells and free themselves. Their second need for food, led Mother Duck to waddle off and get them each a tasty beetle. She dropped one beetle into each of their flat little beaks.

In no time at all they were hungry again, so Mother got some fat juicy worms. These took longer to eat. After that they were sleepy. Mother Duck had worked hard all morning to feed her little ones. She decided to waddle off while they slept and find something to eat for herself.

While she was gone one of the ducklings awoke. His eyes were big and black. He lifted his head to the sky and saw some clouds for the first time. It tickled his fancy and so he jumped up and down with joy. He thought how much fun to be up in the sky and to touch the clouds.

A perfect 'V' glided across the blue. What was it? He strained his eyes and discovered they were birds. They were much bigger than he and the other ducklings. They were even bigger than his Mother.

The duckling knew right then and there that he wanted to fly. He wasn't sure how or when, but he knew he'd find a way. Mother Duck returned shortly. Her feet were wet and she smelled of fish.

"Hello, little Fred," she quacked. He nestled close and looked up in the sky just in time to see the 'V' disappear behind the trees. He didn't say anything about it to Mother. He didn't know what to say. It was just a little secret he decided to keep.

The next morning, Mother Duck woke her ducklings bright and early.

"Today, you are going to learn to swim."

They yawned and quacked about being tired but they followed Mama to the pond. As they walked along, little Fred put his head to the sky in hopes of seeing the marvelous birds again. He held his beak so high that he bumped right into one of his brothers.

"Hey, watch where you're going," squawked Timmy.

"I am watching," Fred dreamily said. "Isn't it wonderful?"

"What?" asked Timmy blankly.

Little Fred didn't say, for he remembered this was his secret. After a few minutes of paddling along, he looked upward again.

"Little Fred, watch where you're going and not the geese in the sky," scolded Mother Duck.

"So, that's what the 'V' is," thought little Fred, "geese."

When they got to the stream, the duck family was excited. This was their first swimming lesson. Fred didn't feel quite the excitement as the others.

"What's so great about being wet and chilly?" he wondered. He felt that the real action was up there soaring in the sky.

"Come along, little Fred," coaxed Mama. "Into the water with you.

"Mama," little Fred said earnestly, "I think I'd rather fly."

"Little Fred, ducks don't do as much flying as swimming and fishing. You've got to get those down pat to survive. Later you can learn to fly when your wings grow bigger."

"All right, Mama." Little Fred got into the water and paddled out to his brothers and sisters.

Mama taught them to move their webbed feet back and forth and how to glide. She also taught them to use their tails for balance when they look for fish under water. For the next few days the duck family spent a lot of time in the pond. Ducking into the water was easy for Fred and so he could spend some time sky gazing as his brothers and sisters worked on their lessons. When each duckling could catch a fish, Mama concluded the lessons.

"Children, you have done wonderfully well, especially you little Fred. You do everything a big duck can do. Swimming wasn't so bad, was it?"

Little Fred beamed with mother's praise. His tail feathers stuck up just a little and his head bobbed a quarter inch higher than before.

"Now, can I learn to fly?" Fred asked eagerly.

"Little Fred, you don't have any grown up feathers. You won't be able to fly until you have long feathers and strong wings like these." She stretched out her beautiful wings for Fred to see.

Fred looked at mother and then at himself. He knew he could fly off the ground a short distance because he already tried.

"When will I be a grown up, Mother?" Fred wanted to know.

"Oh, not too long," assured Mother. "But, I promise you as soon as you are I'll teach you to fly."

Little Fred was disappointed but he knew Mother kept her word. Later, when the others were asleep Little Fred was still thinking about the day that he would fly. Since his thoughts were keeping him awake, he left the nest to take a walk. To his surprise his wings were big and heavy. His feathers were long and quite hard to manage. He heard a cry above him. Looking up he saw the 'Perfect V' glide across the sky.

"Quack, quack, wait for me," called Fred. He gathered up all his energy and ran as fast as he could. He spread his wings as far as possible and found himself soaring upward. He kept flapping his wings and quacking, "Wait for me, wait for me."

The lead goose turned his head and looked back at Fred. He smiled and said, "Hello, little Fred, we've been waiting for you."

Fred could hardly believe it. When he finally caught up with the geese, they glided smoothly together. The lead goose made space for Fred. It seemed they flew for hours.

Fred knew it would soon be morning. He knew too that mother would worry if he were not in the nest when she awakened. He thanked his kind friend explaining why he must go. The leader understood and told Fred they would take him home. Something flew across his face and before he knew it, he was back in his soft nest with the others. His head was soon cuddled into his downy feathers for a sound sleep.

Morning came quickly. When Fred awoke, he immediately looked down at his new feathers. To his dismay they were gone. He had just the little fluffy ones he always had. He was so upset. Why were his feathers gone? Was this just a dream? He was sure what happened the night before was real! A tear started to trickle down his face.

Then little Fred heard a call from above. He looked up. There was the perfect 'V' and they were calling his name.

"Hello, little Fred," the leader called.

"Hello, hello," he quacked back.

That was the last day of little Fred's first spring. His friends, the geese would come every year for the winter and leave at the end of spring. The next year on their return little Fred was full grown. He spent wonderful time flying with them. He never knew how his wings had grown long for one magical night, but he didn't care. He knew it happened!

Seasonal Stories

Halloween

Happy Halloween

by Mary Apple
Ocean City, Maryland
Grade 7, Berlin Middle School

It was late in the small town of Louisville, Maryland when Michelle Condor and I left Katie Talbot's Halloween Party. We decided to walk home because we didn't think it was fair to call our parents out after a busy day of putting up with kids on Halloween. It was unusually dark and cold, and I remember how we shivered as we walked along the lonely lane.

I started to walk faster and I yelled over my shoulder for Michelle to hurry a little. She didn't answer so I looked back. She wasn't there. I came to a complete stop and called her name. I looked into the empty street before me; no answer! I felt panic start to rise up from my stomach. I called again, nothing.

I started to run home telling myself that she probably did the same. I had a strange feeling that someone was watching me. I started running faster, breaking into a hard run. I ran up my driveway as fast as I could. Gasping for air, I fiddled with the key until finally I got it into the lock and opened the door.

Once inside, I threw off my shoes and raced up to my bedroom. Everyone was asleep and I was so tired, I didn't even put on my pajamas. I kept thinking about Michelle and wondering if she was all right. Finally from exhaustion, I dozed off to sleep.

The next day was Saturday and Katie came over. We were concentrating on a game so intently that when the phone rang, we both jumped. I picked up the phone. "Hello," I answered. I heard heavy breathing.

"Michelle, is that you?" I asked nervously. Then a wispy voice started asking me questions like what was I doing and who was home. My parents had always told me never to answer calls like that but I was so scared that I just kept holding on to the receiver. Katie grabbed the phone and hung up. She could tell I was scared stiff. When I could finally speak, I told her about the weird questions. She said it was probably a prank call and to forget it.

A little while later, Katie went home. I went to my room to listen to music. After spending a few minutes searching for my special station, I heard a strange scratching sound. I flipped off the radio and listened. For a moment there was nothing. Then, I heard a thumping sound. I carefully inspected my room and found nothing that could make the noise. Thumping and scratching continued and grew louder. I began tearing my room apart like a maniac but there was nothing. The noise continued.

Dad was at work; Mom was shopping. Neither would be home for at least an hour. I put my hands on my ears, ran out of the house and down the road to Katie's. I knocked but no one was home. I turned to go back to my own house, sensing it would soon be dark. I started to run because I had this strange, terrifying feeling.

On arriving home, I turned the door knob, but the door didn't open. I was locked out of my own house! I hadn't even bothered to close the front door when I left before, so someone else must have done it. Remembering a key in my pocket, with shaking fingers I unlocked the door. When I got inside, I froze. Something seemed different. At first I thought it was something about the furniture but I didn't really know because I was really shaken up. Still my parents weren't home! I couldn't stand it anymore, so I called the police. I told them I felt someone was harassing me. They assured me that they would have someone come out and watch. I hung up,

For the next few days, the harassment continued: noises, phone calls, eerie sounds. Then, I got a call from the police. It had never occurred to me my friends were playing tricks on me. I immediately went to Michelle's house.

"How could you and Katie do this to me?" I screamed at her. "I got really scared by all this stuff."

Michelle apologized and told me that she and Katie didn't think I would get so scared or so mad. I stormed out of her house and into mine.

"What's wrong?" Mom asked.

"Oh, nothing." I didn't want to upset Mom.

In spite of my anger, I knew that this was one Halloween I'd never forget.

The Secret

by Adam Radtke
Ocean City, Maryland
Grade 7, Berlin Middle School

The phone was ringing loudly in the kitchen. Jessica hurried down to get it. "Hello."

"Hey, Jess, what are you doing?" Judy asked in excitement.

"Is this Judy?"

"Yeah, don't tell me you forgot me already."

"No, I didn't," she answered with disinterest.

"Well, I can tell you are really happy to be talking to me."

"Oh, I'm just bored. My parents won't let me go anywhere because I mouthed off to them. Well, let's change the subject. How's your great Uncle Thomas' house? Is it neat?" Jessica asked.

"Oh, it's fine, I guess but it's kind of spooky. What I really wanted was to see if you could stay here with me for a few days until he gets back."

There was silence and then, "Well, I don't know, I'll ask."

Judy could hear a discussion in the background. It was about three minutes before Jess came back on the phone but it wasn't Jess. It was her mother, Ms. Barbara. Sometimes Ms. Barbara was a nice lady and sometimes she seemed strict. Often Jess would have to stay home just because her room was a mess or her homework wasn't done.

"Judy, is your mother home? I'd like to talk to her."

"Hold on, I'll get her." It took Mom about three minutes to come because she was upstairs cleaning the bathroom.

"Hello, Sally, what's this about Jessie spending a few nights?"

"Actually, Barbara, it's almost a week. I'm letting Judy watch Michael from Monday until Friday while I visit my parents. Is that all right with you?"

I could tell Mom wanted to finish the conversation and get back to cleaning but you don't really settle things with Ms. Barbara that quickly. It didn't sound like it was going smoothly. Then, I heard Mom say, "Well, really Barbara, they're seventeen now. I think the two of them together watching Michael will be fine."

Ms. Barbara said she'd think it over and call back. I knew that if Jess wasn't going to come, that there was no way I wanted to stay in that creepy place! Besides, Michael could get on your nerves quite easily.

The phone rang. It was Jessica; her mother gave the OK. That would make things better.

I really hated the idea of staying at Uncle Thomas' house. It was dirty and creepy. I don't know why Mom agreed to house sit for her brother but she did and that was that. I went upstairs to read my book while I waited for Jess to come.

After a while I came back downstairs to get something to eat.

"Mom, where is Michael?" I asked.

"He's picking up his friend. He should be back in a couple of minutes."

Mom was right. Shortly after, Michael walked in with his friend, Dexter. My brother, Michael is only nine years old. His best friend, Dexter is a month older. Michael is a pain in the neck but Dexter is rather nice.

"Hi, Mom," Michael said running into the kitchen. "Hi ya, big jerk," he said to me.

"Michael, you know you shouldn't talk to your sister that way. Now apologize."

"I'm sorry," Michael said.

Dexter came in calmly and quietly. "Hi, Sally." Dexter always calls parents by their first names, even his own parents. Sometimes he may even say their full name. My mother's name is Sally O'Neil and my father's name is David. I don't really like our last name but I absolutely hate Cheryl, which is my middle name.

Soon it was time for dinner. We all sat down to eat. After dinner I went back upstairs to read more of "The Waitress" by R.L. Stine, until Jessica got there. It was about an hour before I heard the doorbell. I quickly ran downstairs.

"I'll get it. I'll get it." I opened the door and there stood Jessica. We hugged each other and quickly went upstairs. Within a few minutes, my mother was calling me. I went downstairs to the kitchen.

"Your father and I are getting ready to go. I want you to take care of Michael and Dexter and be sure they behave. Uncle Thomas will be back either Thursday or Friday. Your father and I will be back by the end of the week. Call us if you need us. There's plenty of food; everything should be all right."

My mother and father hugged me goodbye and then yelled goodbye to Michael. Michael yelled back 'bye' and they were off. It was just about 8:00 p.m. and I went back to Jess.

"Do you want to watch a movie with Dexter and Michael?" I asked.

"Sure," she said. I went over to Michael's room. He and Dexter were playing Monopoly.

"Hey, guys, do you want to watch a movie?" I asked.

"What movie?" Michael asked.

"Um ... a scary movie."

"Do you want to Dexter?" Michael asked.

"Okay," he answered. We all went downstairs to pick out a scary movie. We first looked at *A Nightmare on Elm Street* and then we started to watch *The Howling*. I put the second movie in the VCR and decided to make some popcorn. I came back a few minutes later and discovered that although the movie wasn't scary at first, my brother and Dexter were now covering their ears and eyes. To me it was too bizarre so I decided to go finish my book.

I went up the stairs stretching and yawning. I really wanted to go to bed but I wanted to finish the book too. I jumped onto the bed and began to read. After reading a chapter, I put the book down and tried to plan what we would do during the week.

All of a sudden I heard a weird sound. I decided they were trying to scare me. I headed down to them.

"Why are you guys making those stupid noises?"

"What noises?" Jess asked with a confused look. All of a sudden I heard it again and so did Jessica, Michael and Dexter.

"Where is that coming from?" Michael asked. We all looked around then heard it again.

"I ... I think it's coming from the basement." We walked together toward the basement door and slowly opened it. Michael and Dexter, trying to act bravely, started down the stairs.

"Ha, ha, ha, ha, ha." Michael and Dexter flew up the steps."Ha, ha, ha, ha, haaaa. Hello, Judy." All of a sudden something or someone was talking to me.

"Who is that down there? If you don't tell me who you are, I'm going to call the police."

"Oh, you don't want to do that, dear friend," the voice said. We heard footsteps and saw a black form coming into view. It was a skeleton wearing a wide brim hat with a black robe and cape. The cape was black on the outside and red on the inside. The ghost was holding a cane with a crystal on top.

"Oh, my goodness, I recognize those clothes," I screamed. "It's Uncle Chester!"

"Hello, dear friend," Chester replied.

"What are you doing here; you're dead."

"Yes I am and I want to tell you how I died."

I was so scared I didn't know what to do. I saw a broom and quickly tossed it at Uncle Chester. Then I slammed the basement door and Jessica and I took off for Michael's room where he and Dexter were hiding.

I slammed Michael's door behind us. I could hear the thump of Uncle Chester falling down the stairs.

"What was that?" Michael asked.

"That was Uncle Chester," I said trying to catch my breath. "He was killed when I was a little girl. No one knew why or how but people thought it was for his money."

"I knew I didn't want to come to this house," I wailed. A few minutes later, we heard the noises again.

"I think he's coming back upstairs" said Dexter.

"You're going to pay for that, Judy," Uncle Chester said. "I"m going to get you and your friends too."

"What are we going to do?" I said, panic stricken. Uncle Chester was now pounding on Michael's door. He forced it open.

"Don't hurt us, Uncle Chester," I screamed at him. He broke the door and came pushing in past Jessica and me. He picked up Michael by the shirt. He carried him over to the staircase. Michael never looked so little.

"Don't hurt Michael," I screamed. He threw Michael down the stairs. I charged right into him.

"Why are you trying to hurt us? We didn't do anything to you? You were trying to scare us and I didn't mean to throw the broom." I was hysterical and yet I tried to reason with him.

"Why?" I kept asking and pleading. "Why?"

"This secret can't be kept any longer," he said. "Fifteen years ago, my brother, Tom and I were at a Halloween Party. A wealthy friend of ours loved costume parties and so decided to give the winner, $500,000. I was dressed as I am now and my brother dressed as a pirate. I won the prize and my brother was insanely jealous. One week later, my brother came to my door with a gun and shot me. No one ever found out. Thomas got all my money, this house and everything. This week, I was finally going to get even and Thomas goes away. Worse still, you kids show up and then try to destroy me."

He started after Michael again. I hit him right in the chest with a chair, the first thing I could grab. His old wound started to bleed. I could see blood all over his shirt.

"Maybe what happened to you was wrong," I said. "But what you're doing is equally wrong."

He raised his cane and must have struck me because I found myself moaning on the floor. I opened my mouth to scream but not a sound came out. Jessica stood there petrified. I could see that she was going to get it next. Uncle Chester started toward her.

Somewhere in the distance I heard a loud pounding.

"Oh, thank God," I said.

I awoke in a sweat and went over to open the bedroom door.

"Mom, am I glad to see you. You won't believe what I was dreaming."

All Hallow's Eve

by Michelle Connor
Berlin, Maryland
Grade 7, Berlin Middle School

As summer ended and September began, I was sad to see Sara, my best friend move away. We had been friends since first grade. I couldn't imagine starting another school year without her.

Time moved on and school started for me without Sara's companionship. We called each other and wrote often. One day I received an invitation to Sara's Halloween Party. I was so happy I danced with my cat around the living room. Sara wanted me to come over on the 30th to help her get ready. I was going to stay the whole weekend.

When I arrived at Sara's, she greeted me with a bowl of cookie dough and a wooden spoon and I was put to work right away. She told me that after we made the cookies, we were going to take paper and crayons over to the cemetery to make some etchings of tombstones. Her mother suggested that etchings make a great way to decorate.

We got to the cemetery and opened the old, creaky, iron gate.

"Do you have the paper and black crayons?" Sara asked.

"Right in my back pack," I answered.

We looked at tombstones and a chill went right up my spine. We were looking at a headstone of a person who died on October 30, this same day but about 50 years ago.

"Well, we probably won't find a date closer to Halloween than this," Sara said. "You copy it and I'll look for one more."

Sara went off a little way and I started working. I was almost finished and it was getting to be dusk. I heard a strange sound, like a crying cat.

"Sara, did you hear that?"

"Who wouldn't!" she said. "It was blood curdling." We huddled together and started to leave. As we rushed toward the entrance, we saw an orange light. We also got a whiff of smoke from a new fire.

"Did you see that?" Sara asked in a shaky voice.

"Let's get out of here," I said. "This looks like some kind of cult activity."

We could see a group of teenagers and they were gathered around a small coffin. They had just dug up a tiny grave.

"This is sickening," I whispered to Sara. Just then I saw them pick up a black cat who was screeching something awful. A girl had a pair of clippers in her hand and I dreaded to think of what she might be going to do.

"Oh, please, don't let them see us," I pleaded to myself. Too late, they spotted us. We ran but they caught Sara. I wanted to run forever, but instead I turned around to see what they were going to do to her. One of the boys was holding Sara. I flashed my flashlight into his eyes and he yelled to the others to get me. Again I ran, this time like a speeding bullet.

I got to the gate but couldn't open it. I leaped over it and ran for the nearest house. I pounded frantically on the door. A young lady came to the door.

"Quick," I said. "I have to call the police." I was gasping for air and could hardly get the words out. "My friend is in trouble in the cemetery; teens grabbed her," I said.

The police came quickly and surrounded the group. Sara was on the ground. My heart started pounding, I thought she was dead. Then she moaned. She was badly bruised but okay. The teens were all arrested and we later learned that they weren't from around here.

We had to cancel the Halloween Party but I did spend the weekend at Sara's. We won't forget this horrible *All Hallow's Eve* for a horribly long time.

Seasonal Stories

Christmas

The Greatest Gift of All

Maura Doyle
Cockeysville, Maryland
Grade 8, Maryvale

"Hello, I'm a Dalmatian, but don't have any distinctively beautiful spots. I guess that's how I got the name Bozo."

"My name is Fluffy and I don't want to appear rude but I am rather busy getting ready for Sunday," the white French poodle responded.

"What's so very special about Sunday?" asked Bozo. "Sunday is 'People Day.' I must be excused, Bozo. It's time for me to put in my curlers. I do want to look my best," said Fluffy Poodle, with a warm and cordial, southern accent.

Bozo soon found out that on Sundays many families come into the pound to choose a pet. When

Sunday came, Bozo understood more clearly. A very friendly family came and wanted Fluffy. But, Sunday after Sunday no one chose Bozo.

Miles away, a little boy named Jeffrey Johnson was sitting on his bed and thinking about what he wanted for Christmas. Jeffrey, crippled from birth, thought it would be great to have a puppy. A puppy could play with him, running and fetching, and sometimes curl up on his lap. Jeffrey asked his Mom to go to the pound on Sunday.

Sunday came and Jeffrey decided to dress extra special in his white shirt, blue pants, paisley tie and blue sport coat. He and Mom got into the car and drove off. First to the Pizza Hut, one of their favorite places, then on they drove to the pound.

Mrs. Fruiter showed Jeffrey all the dogs in the pound. She explained that this was a Dalmatian that had few spots. Jeffrey who learned early on, not to 'judge a book by its cover' immediately took to Bozo. Perhaps it was because the dog wasn't perfect that Jeffrey liked him.

Bozo barked good-bye to Holly, Hippie, Boogie, and Candy, dog friends at the pound. Bozo and Jeffrey couldn't wait to get home. Tomorrow was

Christmas Eve. Both Jeffrey and Bozo had someone special.

Jeffrey didn't think Bozo was an appropriate name for a dog who was such a special friend. "Buddy, will be your name," Jeffrey decided. "You are my buddy and you always will be."

Together Jeffrey and Buddy put milk and cookies out for Santa and then sat together under the Christmas Tree. Mother was very pleased to see her little boy feeling so happy. She sat contentedly in her chair. She took out a pen and her feelings just flowed onto the paper. This is what she wrote.

Twas the night before Christmas
and what do we see?
Jeffrey and Buddy cuddled under the tree.
No greater gift could they give each other
But the gift of love to one another.

A Christmas Surprise

by Allison Gidel
Cockeysville, Maryland
Grade 8, Maryvale

It was almost Christmas and Kelly felt so excited. She and her mother just finished last minute decorating. The last batch of cookies in the oven gave off wonderful smells through the house.

"Have you written your list to Santa yet?"

"No," Kelly responded. "I'll write it now." On her new Dalmatian decorated stationery, Kelly wrote her letter.

Dear Santa,

I would like you to bring a teddy bear, a doll with red curls, a pair of roller blades, a memory game and a surprise gift. I also think it would be fun to find a surprise under the tree, something that I didn't think of, but a present that you know I'll like.

Thank you, Santa, for making me and so many children happy each year.

Love,
Kelly

The next day Kelly and Mom enjoyed shopping. They stopped to look in all the store windows. Kelly was trying to imagine her surprise gift. She wondered about Santa's thoughts as he read her letter.

"This is so exciting," Kelly almost said out loud. Kelly reminded Mom to buy cat food so they stopped at the pet store. As Mom picked out the food and paid for it, Kelly wandered around looking at all the animals.

Kelly always liked dogs so she wandered over to the puppies. There she saw the cutest little brown puppy peeking its face out of the cage. Kelly walked over and the pup immediately started yelping.

"What's the matter with you, today?" asked Kelly. As she went nearer, the puppy licked her extended hand. Kelly wanted to take the little pup home with her. She could tell the puppy wanted to go with her too.

"It looks like you have made a new friend," said Mom.

"Oh, Mom, isn't she darling? I'd love to take her home with us. Do you think we could?"

"Well, honey, we already have a cat. Cats and dogs don't always get along," Mom said. "I have to admit though, she's very lovable."

Kelly reluctantly said good-bye to the puppy and she and Mom walked out of the shop. Kelly kept looking back and the young dog continued yelping.

The next day was Christmas Eve. Kelly felt excited and a new blanket of snow added to the feeling. As Kelly played in the snow, she couldn't help thinking about Santa and the toys she would find on Christmas morning. For a while, she and her next door friend, Amy played Santa delivering presents. That was fun. Then Mother called her in to get ready to go to Grandma's house.

It was a family tradition that on Christmas Eve the family would have dinner with their grandparents. Kelly liked this because everyone was in a festive mood. All of her aunts, uncles and cousins came. They took lots of pictures and sang Christmas Carols around the fireplace. Finally, Grandpa would read *The Night Before Christmas* by Clement Moore. That was the signal that it was time to go home and get ready for bed.

When they got home, Kelly put out cookies and milk for Santa. She kissed Mom and Dad and ran upstairs to wait for Santa. Falling asleep on Christmas Eve was always hard. It seemed to take forever but finally she dreamed of Santa and her surprise present. She was just ready to open it, when she awoke.

"Mom, Dad," Kelly ran to her parents' bedroom. "Wake up, it's Christmas."

They hugged each other and then rushed downstairs. Kelly saw her pile of gifts immediately. There was a teddy bear sitting on top of gaily decorated boxes. It was fun tearing open the packages. New roller blades, the red-haired doll, a new paint smock, a memory game, a jump rope, Chinese checkers and red shoes were all for her. It was wonderful!

Kelly looked around to see if there was one more present with a note from Santa. She was hoping that he didn't forget a special surprise. She didn't see anything else. She felt a bit disappointed but as she looked at all the nice things she knew she had received plenty.

"Maybe Santa didn't have time for a surprise this year," she thought. "I'll ask him to do it next year."

Kelly, Mom and Dad went out into the kitchen for a yummy breakfast of western omelet and danish. Kelly decided that she must have the best Mom and Dad in the whole world. They told her that's how they felt about her too.

She went upstairs to get dressed for church and saw something small and white on the bed. It was a note. She picked it up and read it.

Dear Kelly,
You asked me for a surprise gift. I have one for you. Go out to the garage and you will find your present. I hope you like it.

Love,
Santa Claus

P.S.
Thanks for being such a good girl. You give your parents so much joy. Thanks also for the snack.

Kelly flew down the steps calling to Mom and Dad as she ran. "There's a surprise in the garage from Santa. Let's go look."

She raced outside with her parents following close on her heels. The first thing she saw was a huge red bow. Then she realized it was attached to a cage. There was the puppy she saw in the pet store.

"Oh, wow, the puppy!" She scooped him up into her arms.

"How did Santa know?"

"Santa's been watching you," said Dad.

"Oh, Santa, what a Christmas surprise!" 

A Christmas Wish

by Kathryn A. Lafferty
Reisterstown, Maryland
Grade 8, Maryvale

It was Thursday, December 21, and young Jimmy was getting up and preparing himself for school. The air was full of excitement. This was the last day of school at Wickermill Elementary before the Christmas holidays. Jimmy went into the bathroom to wash his face and to brush his teeth.

"Hey, Jimmy, watch it," cried Beth, his older sister. "You're not the only one in this bathroom, you know."

Beth was one of Jimmy's sisters. He had another sister, Marla and a brother, David. Jimmy was the youngest.

"Sorry, Beth, I didn't mean to bump you, honest!"

"Okay, but be more careful Jimmy," said Beth. "I almost got toothpaste all over me."

"Beth, Marla, David and Jimmy, breakfast is ready." Mother always called them according to age.

"Coming," they answered in unison. This was a routine call each morning and the children were used to it.

Mrs. Jenkins was a single mother. Mr. Jenkins passed away suddenly, soon after Jimmy was born. The children were very close to their mother and to each other. Everyone who knew the Jenkins family was struck by their obvious love for each other.

After breakfast, the kids kissed Mom and then headed to school. First they walked Jimmy to his school and then the other three headed over to the high school about four blocks away.

"Hey, Jimmy, wait up," bellowed Pete Connors, Jimmy's best friend. Together they went into the first grade classroom.

When recess finally rolled around, all the kids in Mrs. Whiley's class raced for the playground. All but Jimmy, he was choo-chooing along like an engine. He sang his favorite song, the one he heard the kids sing as they played jump rope.

Engine-Engine-Number-Nine
Steaming down the New York line.
If the train falls off the track
Pick it up and put it back.

Some of the fourth grade girls decided to tease Jimmy.

"Oh, Jimmy," one of them called."We have a song for you." They started to sing.

Engine-Engine-Number-Nine
Rolling down the garbage line.
If the train falls off the track,
Pick it up and break your back.

"Oh, those stupid girls, who needs them?" thought Jimmy. Then he spotted Pete Connors and the two of them continued playing train.

The Christmas Play filled the final hours and then D-I-N-N-G! The final bell clanged and vacation began.

"Yea!" thought Jimmy. "Christmas is almost here."

He shoved his books into his locker and ran to meet up with Pete.

"Where are you going in such a hurry?" Jimmy wanted to know.

"The baseball game out in the back alley," said Pete, "did you remember?"

"Oh, yea!" said Jimmy. So off they went to the alley. They played for an hour or more and it was final bats for Jimmy's team. They needed a hit to score.

"Come, on Jimmy, hit it hard," the boys yelled. He gave a mighty swing and missed. Swish! Swish! Two more times he missed.

"Boo, Jimmy can't hit. boo," some of the boys hissed.

Jimmy was so upset, he ran right home. That night he kept hearing those *boos* even in his sleep. "I'll show them," he was muttering.

Finally, Christmas Eve arrived.

"Beth, Marla, David, Jimmy, time for breakfast."

"Coming."

"I'll race you to the kitchen," David challenged.

"Okay," answered Jimmy.

After breakfast, the family went into town to see all the Christmas decorations. Garlands stretched from one side of the mall to the other. Reindeer and sleigh pranced on top of the Hecht's Department Store. Bells were ringing as the Salvation Army made its last collections. Then Jimmy saw something that made his face light up.

"Mom, look! It's Engine-Engine-Number-Nine! That's what I want for Christmas. Can I have it, Mom? Can I have it? Huh? Huh?"

"It's too expensive for me, Jimmy. You'd better ask Santa." Mother felt terrible but that's all she could say.

Jimmy didn't want to leave the window when the family started walking toward the next shop. He was studying the little engine and imagining all kinds of games to play with it.

"Come on, Jimmy, it's time to go," called Mrs. Jenkins.

They finished their tour of the mall and then went home for lunch.

"A special lunch for special kids," sang Mom. She poured out hot cider and gave them all tuna and chips. For dessert, they ate homemade sugar cookies from Grandmom.

The afternoon went by quickly as they helped set up the tree and put out the Christmas Nativity set. All these things Mama had in her house when she was growing up. Each year they were carefully unwrapped and the living room was transformed into the home of Mama's childhood. It was wonderful for each of them. Mama's only regret was that she could not do more for them.

Bedtime finally arrived. Jimmy did not get to sleep easily. Christmas excitement keeps children awake and so it did for Jimmy. He wondered what Santa would bring. He was hoping to see Santa this year. He kept an ear alerted for the reindeer but before he heard him, he finally fell asleep.

"Mom," wake up called the Jenkins children.

"It's Christmas! Santa came!" shouted Jimmy.

"Come on everyone," Mother replied. "Let's go downstairs."

The magic of the decorated Christmas tree and the presents gaily wrapped under it thrilled all of them. They quickly unwrapped their presents crying out their pleasure. Everyone seemed happy and Jimmy too. But after he unwrapped his last present he burst out crying.

"Why doesn't Santa like me?" he asked through his sobs.

"Why, Jimmy, why would you say something like that?" replied Mother. She picked him up in her arms and tried to make sense of it.

"Santa ... Santa ... he ... he ... didn't bring me Engine-Engine-Number Nine," he finally blurted out.

"Oh, Jimmy," Mother comforted him. "Santa can't bring you everything. He does what he can for all little girls and boys. I know Santa loves you very much."

"Pete says, there is no Santa," Jimmy cried.

"Do you believe Pete?" asked Mom.

"I guess not," said Jimmy.

"Come on kids," said Mama. "Let's play with Jimmy's new toys. And David, put on some Christmas music, will you?"

It was a good day after all. The Jenkins family knew how to play together and that's what they did. After a while, they went outside to build a snowman. On the way out the door, Jimmy thought he heard bells. Then he saw something next to the snowman they made yesterday. It was a box with a bow and a tag that said, 'Jimmy'. He quickly took the lid off the box and found a note inside.

Dear Jimmy,
Thanks for believing in me.
Love, Santa

Jimmy tore back the paper. There, red and shiny was Engine-Engine-Number-Nine.

A

One Act

Play

(Ilustrations by Rosanna Graf)

The Foods That Came Alive

A One Act Play

by Rosanna Graf
Towson, Maryland
Grade 1, Home Schooling

Characters: Fairy
Broccoli
Peanut
Milk
Onion
Salad
Potato
Orange Juice

Setting - One morning in the World of Really Real, a place children always know, a very unusual thing happened right in the kitchen.

Costumes -Each food character is dressed in the typical color of the food. The fairy is dressed in a long dress with a matching bonnet.

Fairy: I am the Food Fairy who watches over Good Foods. (She takes off her bonnet and places it on a chair.) Whenever there are children who like the foods very much, I bring them to life for a short visit into the world of humans. The foods think its fun for a few hours. On this very special day there are seven lively foods in conversation. Come and listen. (She exits.)

Broccoli: Whew! This is fun! (Hands on hips.) Now what am I supposed to do? (He notices that he is wearing clothes.) Look! My green body has changed. I now have green shoes, green pants, green shirt and a green sweater. (He picks up a bonnet from a chair.) What in the world is this thing? Let me ask my friend, Peanut what it is. (He calls.) Oh, Peanut!

Peanut: Yes.

Broccoli: What is this thing? (He shows him the bonnet.)

Peanut: (Shrugging his shoulders.) I don't know. I'm still quite small and haven't seen much. Let me think. Oh, yes, it's for your head. I think ... I think ... uh ... I think it's a bootie bonnet.

Broccoli: A bootie bonnet?

Peanut: Well, wait, I'm not quite sure! (He scratches his head.) Let me ask my friend, Milk. He gets around more than I do. (He calls.) Milk, Milk.

Broccoli: (Adds in on the calling.) Oh, Milk ...

Milk: (Comes out flexing his muscles.) Yes, what is it?

Peanut: Broccoli and I want to know what this thing is. Peanut thinks its something to be worn on a human head. (Broccoli holds out the bonnet.)

Milk: (Laughing.) Oh too bad lettuce isn't here. She knows about heads. (Laughs again at his own joke.) Hmmm, Let's see ... a thing you wear on your head ... yes ... hmmmm ... I think I've seen babies wear them.

Peanut: I thought I heard someone call it a bootie bonnet, but I'm not sure.

Milk: A bootie bonnet? No, no, that's not it! I'm not sure, but that doesn't sound right. They put the bonnets on their heads and say, ... let's see. (Milk scratches his head.) What do mothers say to their babies? I've heard them say things like wanna bottle and warm formula to the baby. (Cradles the bonnet in his arm pretending it's a baby and then gives an imaginary bottle to it.) Maybe it's a formula bonnet. Well, I think it's either called a wanna bottle or a formula bonnet.

Onion: (Comes out with hands up like a traffic cop.) I don't want to make anyone cry like I've done in the past, but I think you're all wrong. I've heard and seen a lot of crying. I've seen mothers comfort babies too. (Onion takes the bonnet and rocks it back and forth.) I think they call this a lullaby bonnet.

Salad: No, no, no! (Comes out with a firm determination.) None of you are right! Talk about being mixed up. (Throws hands up in the air.) You're tossing around too many ideas. Now, I agree with onion that mothers can get babies to stop crying sometimes with a lullaby but not always. Mothers also ask crying babies, (Salad says softly.) are you hungry? (Takes the bonnet and pretends to be feeding the bonnet like it's a baby.) Then they give them something to eat. So, Broccoli, what you are wearing on your head is called a hungry bonnet. (Hands bonnet back to Broccoli.)

Broccoli: Really? Why ... why ... thank you ... (Then he looks around and says hesitantly.) I don't know what to think ... I mean ... well ... everyone says they are right and yet no one has agreed. How will I know who is correct?

Potato: Listen to me. I've been peeled, washed, cooked, mashed, french fried and baked. (Moves body as if being washed, peeled etc.) I have a lot of experience. Even though I never wore anything on my head, I have been around people who did. The people who worked with me were chefs. I think what you wear on your head is called a chef's bonnet.

<u>Orange Juice</u>: (Fluffs up his orange clothes.) Well, I know a lot about Vitamin C ... and I don't know anything about clothes. (Hands on hips.) But I am bright like the sun, and may give some light on the subject. (Fluffs clothes again.) One thing I did notice is everyone of you has been using the same word, bonnet. So, I think that all of you may be right. (Hands outstretched to all of them.) What you wear on your head may simply be called a bonnet.

<u>Everybody starts talking at once:</u> (They laugh at orange juice and they argue at the same time.) No, no! that couldn't be right. You're wrong. You're wrong ... It's too plain. It has to be more than that. It's a ... (They each say the name they used before.)

<u>Fairy:</u> (Enters and walks over to Broccoli.) My goodness, excuse me my nourishing friends, I thought I left my bonnet behind, and here it is. (She takes the bonnet from broccoli and puts it on her head.) I feel so undressed without my bonnet. (Then she waves and leaves.)

Everyone laughs!

TEACHER ACKNOWLEDGEMENTS

Story telling is an art that only some people may possess but all people may enjoy. In this first contest and subsequent publication of *Stories for Children by Children,* it is the magic of story that binds together children of all ages. We wish to acknowledge and thank all those teachers who encouraged their students to become story tellers and to write their stories for others to read and enjoy.

Susan Barker, Pine Grove Elementary, Baltimore

Sally Bowen, Maryvale Prep, Brooklandville

Jeanine Brizendine, Catonsville Elem., Catonsville

Katy Dallam, Harford Day School, BelAir

Barbara Dickman, Dasher Green Elem., Columbia

Myrna Dyson, Berlin Middle School, Berlin

Cyrilla Hergenhan, Catonsville Elem., Catonsville

Marianne Kendrick, Oak Hill Elem., Severna Park

Mary Margaret King, The Calverton, Huntington

Teresa Koogle, Kingsville Elem., Kingsville

Nancy Lake, Faith Baptist School, Salisbury

Barbara Lorton, Beach El., Chesapeake Beach

Janet Murray, St. Augustine School, Elkridge

Carolyn Mulligan, St. Augustine School, Elkridge

Susan Polen, St. Michael Elem., St Michaels

Helen Seawell, Plumpoint Middle, Huntington

Suzanne Steinke, Hillcrest Elem., Catonsville

Charlene Stine, Red House Run, Baltimore

Victoria Szabo, Mt. de Sales Academy, Catonsville

Cathy Urban, St. Clement School, Rosedale

Joan Varholy, Bishop John Neumann, Baltimore

Stephanie Zenger, Chesapeake HS, A A County

Elizabeth Seton High School, Bladensburg

ANNUAL WRITING CONTEST

Vangar Publishers invite all students ages 5 to 15 years old to submit original stories. The annual contest is held November 15 to February 15. Submissions are accepted only within that time period each year. A student may submit only one entry per year. They must use the official dated entry form but that form may be duplicated for convenience.

Students whose stories are chosen for publication will receive a trophy and three books in which their stories appear. The awards will be made at a school assembly wherever that is agreeable to the school administration. Official notice of awards and publication will be mailed annually to those students and/or schools sending submissions. All students who send stories will be acknowledged.

Official rules and entry forms may be received from **Stories for Children by Children**

Vangar Publishers

420 Hillen Road

Towson, MD 21286